PEER REVIEW

Charleston Briefings: Trending Topics for Information Professionals is a thought-provoking series of brief books concerning innovation in the sphere of libraries, publishing, and technology in scholarly communication. The briefings, growing out of the vital conversations characteristic of the Charleston Conference and *Against the Grain*, will offer valuable insights into the trends shaping our professional lives and the institutions in which we work.

The *Charleston Briefings* are written by authorities who provide an effective, readable overview of their topics—not an academic monograph. The intended audience is busy nonspecialist readers who want to be informed concerning important issues in our industry in an accessible and timely manner.

Matthew Ismail, Editor in Chief

PEER REVIEW

Reform and Renewal in Scientific Publishing

ADAM ETKIN,
THOMAS GASTON,
AND JASON ROBERTS

Published in the United States of America by
ATG LLC (Media)
Manufactured in the United States of America

DOI: http://dx.doi.org/10.3998/mpub.9944026

ISBN 978-1-941269-14-5 (paper)
ISBN 978-1-941269-18-3 (e-book)

www.against-the-grain.com

CONTENTS

INTRODUCTION

Misunderstandings are rife regarding what exactly peer review is and the purpose it is intended to serve. There are many variations of peer review, each with
its own set of advantages and disadvantages. While peer review continues to
evolve alongside the scholarly publishing and academic community it serves,
it is clear that the large majority of researchers continue to believe the review
system is a linchpin of scientific communication. In this short book, we will
provide an overview of the history of peer review, types of peer review, challenges to the system, and possible future developments.

HISTORY OF PEER REVIEW

EARLY PEER REVIEW

To understand how we have arrived at a self-regulating system that simultaneously validates results, theories, and opinions; offers suggestions for improving what is published; and ultimately determines what gets published within a given field's definitive body of literature, we need to first consider the history of peer review. It is a history that is both old (in its inception) and, perhaps surprisingly, somewhat modern in its execution, with many journals and periodicals formally instituting a structure of review that calls on acknowledged experts in the field to assess a manuscript submission only in the last five decades.

In 1662, the Royal Society of London was founded by a cadre of curious men who were dedicated both to science and to the acquaintance of like-minded scientific thinkers. A contemporary planning document from 1660 had called for the formation of a "'College for the Promoting of Physico-Mathematical Experimental Learning,' which would meet weekly to discuss science and run experiments" ("Prince of Wales"), and this gives us a solid sense of the intellectual concerns of those founding members. The men of the Royal Society were dedicated not only to meeting in person but also to the communication of scientific knowledge more broadly, and in 1665, they founded the journal *Philosophical Transactions*, usually regarded as the earliest academic journal, with this aim in mind. This earliest society journal's full title was *Philosophical Transactions, Giving some Account of the present*

Undertakings, Studies, and Labours of the Ingenious in many considerable parts of the World, which emphasizes that its mission was not limited to the members residing in London. Gradually, similar-minded publications began to emerge. In 1699, for example, the Académie Royale des Sciences of Paris was founded with similar aims, and this society also created its own publication, the *Journal des Sçavans*.

Today we might ask whether *Philosophical Transactions* was peer-reviewed on the assumption that peer review is the process that makes a journal scientific or results and theories valid rather than a matter of opinion or conjecture. And indeed, peer review—or the collegial process whereby scholars evaluate research papers independently before publication is granted in a particular journal—is commonly assumed to have originated with the emergence of these academic societies and the scientific journals they founded (Hames; for more on the history of peer review, see Fyfe; Kronick; Fitzpatrick). Allowing its broadest definition, "peer review can be said to have existed ever since people began to identify and communicate what they thought was new knowledge" (Kronick 1321). Even prior to the formation of the learned societies, early scientists corresponded among their peers with the intention of soliciting comments and critique on their work. *Philosophical Transactions* and its ilk sought to improve and, to a certain degree, replace this previous practice of reporting on scientific observations and discoveries by personal correspondence. Yet while an element of selection (in the form of acceptance or rejection) was implicit in the operation of these early scientific journals, it would be far from accurate to equate that selection process with peer review as we know it today.

The founding editor of *Philosophical Transactions*, Henry Oldenburg, actively gathered content for the journal from contemporaneously published pamphlets, from meetings of the Royal Society, and from his own correspondence. Unlike modern editors, he was not deluged by unsolicited submissions and his role did not require him to prioritize articles for impact or originality. There was a certain level of scrutiny of some of the scientific reports, inasmuch as research findings were presented and discussed at meetings of the Royal Society. But it is somewhat inaccurate to describe material published in *Philosophical Transactions* as peer-reviewed in the modern sense of the term.

Later journals would come to adopt broader peer review practices, such as the creation of an editorial team at the *Journal des Sçavans* (as opposed to a solitary editor making decisions and more akin to the currently understood notion of an editorial board). This step, instituted after 1701, was rendered necessary by the breadth of fields covered in that publication. Later still, the Royal Society of Edinburgh began to solicit reviews from knowledgeable members for contributions to *Medical Essays and Observations* (1731). The preface to that journal stated, "Memoirs sent by correspondence are distributed according to the subject matter to those members who are most versed in these matters. The report of their identity is not known to the author." Not only is this an early description of a peer review process; it represents one of the first declarations of what we would call a "blinded peer review" approach, whereby the author's identity would remain obscured to the reviewer, presumably on the grounds of ensuring a fair and unbiased peer review.

In 1752, the Royal Society of London appointed the Committee of Papers to evaluate potential contributions. Similarly, the *Philosophical Magazine*, founded in 1798, originally had a single editor but by the 1850s was run by a five-man editorial team to ensure comprehensive coverage of various disciplines. However, none of these arrangements constituted what we understand as "peer review" today—that is, systematic procedures for independent review by experts in the field. The Royal Society's Committee of Papers sought to ensure some level of control by the society regarding what appeared in the pages of *Philosophical Transactions*. The committee format was intended to remove the onus of selection from a single individual and limit the danger of bias or prejudice.

Yet the Royal Society recognized that its committee could not guarantee the validity of everything *Philosophical Transactions* published, and the journal carried a statement in each issue to the effect that "the certainty of the facts, or propriety of the reasonings . . . must still rest on the credit or judgment of their respective authors." It is interesting to note that the Académie Royale des Sciences in Paris did attempt to test the validity of research findings. The organization had a remit from the Crown to assess the merits of inventions and discoveries, and the committees appointed to investigate these sought to replicate and test research findings. This level of validation went far beyond what is expected (or possible) with modern peer review, and by the 1830s, this process had been abandoned as being too time-consuming (Fyfe).

Interestingly, in clinical medical publishing at least, there is now a movement back toward reproducing results, principally through the provision and sharing of data and the drive to improve the reporting of methods. Nevertheless, this is still some way short of what was undertaken by the Académie Royale des Sciences.

The next stage in the evolution of peer review was the move from in-house editorial panels or committees to truly independent reports on submissions. This practice emerged among several learned societies in the early 19th century. In 1831, the Royal Society experimented with jointly authored reports—a precursor of modern ideas about collaborative peer review—but from 1832 onward, the Committee of Papers was soliciting independently written reports (Fyfe). This process quickly became part of the standard procedure for publication at learned societies. The collaborative aspect of peer review arose again when George Gabriel Stokes was secretary of the Royal Society (1854–85). Stokes gave considerable attention to mediation of the discourse between reviewers and authors to improve the text. Simultaneously, Ernest Hart, the editor of the *British Medical Journal* (*BMJ*; 1868–98), used a similar model of peer review and extolled its virtues, though complaining of the effort it required.

Yet despite these early examples of the independent review of papers, many journals in the 19th century ignored independent review altogether, and peer review as we understand it today was far from routine until as recent as the mid-20th century. Thomas Wakley, for example, who founded the *Lancet* in 1823, had little appreciation of review or incentive to use peer review, not least because he wrote much of the content himself (Burnham). *Physical Review* introduced a peer-review process in the early 1930s, but the process was mostly employed when the editor required a second opinion. Neither *Science* nor the *Journal of the American Medical Association* (*JAMA*) used outside reviewers until the 1940s (Fitzpatrick). The founding editor of *Nature*, Norman Lockyer, made most of the editorial decisions himself, only seeking additional opinions from his contacts when necessary. *Nature*, in fact, did not adopt a formal peer-review process until 1967.

Illustrative of the exception rather than the rule of utilizing external expert opinion, it is interesting to note that Albert Einstein published more than 300 articles between 1901 and 1955, but it is likely that only one of those was ever subject to peer review (Kennefick). Einstein sent a letter to the editor of a journal taking umbrage with the fact that his work had been subjected to review by an unknown scholar, a process he seemed to regard as rather underhanded:

Dear Sir,

We (Mr. Rosen and I) had sent you our manuscript for publication and had not authorized you to show it to specialists before it is printed. I see no reason to address the—in any case erroneous—comments of your anonymous expert. On the basis of this incident I prefer to publish the paper elsewhere.

Respectfully,

P.S. Mr. Rosen, who has left for the Soviet Union, has authorized me to represent him in this matter.

Tellingly, however, it should be noted that Einstein went on to publish the same paper in another journal, incorporating revisions based on the comments by the original reviewer. Some feel that these revisions might have saved him from public embarrassment and evidently show the value of peer-based critique, even if that usefulness was perhaps not appreciated.

It is significant to note that according to the *Oxford English Dictionary,* the term "peer review" was not used in print until 1967 (Fyfe). The frequent use of the term from the 1970s onward parallels the widespread use of peer review, both for nonsociety journals and for research grant applications. Since then, peer review has become standard practice across scholarly publishing and the "peer-reviewed" label has become a hallmark of genuine science and knowledge.

WHY DID PEER REVIEW EMERGE?

It is quite evident that "peer review, the process by which material submitted for publication is critically assessed by external experts . . . was introduced into different journals at different times and in different ways, often dependent on the chief editor at the time" (Hames). There had been little incentive for early journal editors to adopt peer review because, as noted previously, they often gathered, and even wrote, much of the content themselves. There might also have been an element of editorial pride involved: editors were often loath to admit that they required the opinions of others to determine what to publish (Burnham).

The development of peer review has also mirrored the evolution of scholarly journals. Early journals were often the communication vehicles of particular learned societies, employed to disseminate news and information relevant to members of the organization. Members of societies often asserted their expectation that they would be published in their society's journal. Frequently journals were seen more as media for mass communication than as arbiters of accuracy in science (Nielsen). Other journals were personal organs of their editors or were institutional proceedings to publish the research undertaken at a given research establishment. Editors often viewed their primary role as educators—as disseminators of information—rather than as guardians of the scientific literature. There was, therefore, less expectation for the independence of the journal's content.

Indeed, not only were many early journals not peer reviewed, but they made no claim to have either verified or authenticated the research they published. Denis de Sallo, the first editor of *Journal des Sçavans*, wrote in 1699, "We aim to report the ideas of others without guaranteeing them" (Rennie, "Editorial Peer Review" 2). The Royal Society of Edinburgh issued the following statement concerning its publications:

> The sanction which the Society gives to the work now published under its auspices, extends only to the novelty, ingenuity or importance of the several memoirs which it contains.
>
> Responsibility concerning the truth of facts, the soundness of reasoning, in the accuracy of calculations is wholly disclaimed: and must rest alone, on the knowledge, judgement, or ability of the authors who have respectfully furnished such communications.

Similarly, the Literary and Philosophical Society of Manchester, while not depending on a single editor to determine what was to be published, noted in 1785 that "a majority of votes, delivered by ballot, is not an infallible test in literary or philosophical productions" (Rennie, "Editorial Peer Review" 2). These examples illustrate that even where editors were employing committees, editorial panels, or external reviewers, it was primarily to assist with the selection of manuscripts, not to endorse what was being published.

So while these early journal editors had little incentive to be selective, by the mid-20th century, as the flow of unsolicited articles grew, the need to filter submissions increased as journals, particularly in the predigital age, had to deal with the cost limitations determining how much material could be published. Quality thresholds emerged in response. Those journals seeking to set a high standard for quality research in their fields enforced low acceptance rates to maintain the perceived quality of their content. To achieve such an objective, journals quickly began to rely on reviewers to help identify the small proportion of submissions they preferred to publish (Hames; Burnham; Nielsen).

Beyond the shift toward journals offering validation through publication and some journals taking the lead on delineating and imposing quality thresholds, another factor to consider in the development of peer review is the fact that increased scientific specialization, and the associated increased depth of accumulated knowledge, has made it impossible for a single editor to master all areas of one field. Even with the contemporary expansion of specialized journal publishing, with the publication of journals dedicated to subdisciplines, it is still difficult for a journal editor to be suitably competent to review all submissions. Inevitably, editors have been compelled to reach out to those more qualified to assess the quality of what has been written.

We can also see that changes in technology have made systematic peer review feasible. Prior to the development of carbon paper in the 1890s, and later photocopies in 1959, it was very labor intensive to produce multiple copies of manuscripts to send out for independent review. It is these changes in technology—culminating in the Internet and modern online submission and peer-review systems such as Editorial Manager, ScholarOne, and eJournalPress—that have made peer review by multiple experts both practical and obtainable to journals of all sizes.

It is also clear that changes in the nature of research have required a shift in the way content is selected for publication. Medical publication, for example, has moved from disseminating case history to reporting research conducted by randomized trials (Rennie). As research methodologies and study designs have become ever more technical, the need for specialist assessment has increased.

Fyfe (2015) writes, "The various research teams looking into the history of peer review, including my own, do not yet know enough about why the post-war expansion of scientific research, on both sides of the Atlantic, led to the transformation of refereeing into 'peer review,' or why it then came to dominate the evaluation of scholarly research." Rennie (1999) cites Robin Fox, who, recalling when Ian Munro took over as editor of the *Lancet* in 1976, wrote, "Doctors were becoming reluctant even to cast an eye on research papers that did not bear the 'pass' sticker of peer review" (Rennie). This perception of peer review as the means to distinguish which published material is worthy of consideration dramatically changed the impetus to peer review. It became nearly impossible to be taken seriously as an academic publication without the hallmark of peer review, and thus operating peer review became a reputational and commercial necessity.

This impetus was also increased by the criteria used by institutions to assess potential applicants to academic positions and by funding bodies to award research grants. The motto "publish or perish" for postdocs seeking their first appointment refers only to publication in peer-reviewed journals. Similarly, the assessments by funding bodies, such as the Research Excellence Framework, currently only consider articles published in peer-reviewed journals. Such developments have enforced the ubiquity of peer review in academic publishing but were perhaps secondary to the widespread adoption of peer review.

Interestingly, after reaching a point whereby journals have come to be seen as arbiters of quality and validation through the imposition of peer review, the now almost reflexive notion of journals providing a seal of approval has been recently questioned on two fronts. The first concerns examples of utterly inadequate, or perfunctory, peer review coming to light. The second concerns the rapid proliferation of opportunistic—and almost always exploitative—publications called "predatory journals," titles that give the appearance of offering peer review but in fact do nothing of the sort. These issues we will return to later in discussing the current challenges confronting modern peer review, but they are illustrative of the fact that the relationship between journals and peer review continues to evolve.

WHAT IS PEER REVIEW?

The term "peer review" means different things to different people and in different contexts. In its most basic sense, peer review is simply the evaluation of one's work by one's peers. What distinguishes peer review in the realm of scholarly communication from simply asking for the opinion of your friends, family, or coworkers, however, is that it is a more formal mechanism—sometimes blinded, sometimes not—whereby an official decision is made to designate which peers should be asked to assess a body of work. Within academia and other research milieus, the identity of that additional party varies. The peer reviewer could be a grant-awarding body, a research ethics committee, or a journal. (Though books also constitute a great deal of peer-reviewed, research-directed publishing, this book primarily concerns itself with the work of scientific or research journals.)

Peer review typically serves two purposes:

1. To function as a gatekeeper, determining which papers should be accepted for publication and thus become a part of the body of literature for a specific field of study.
2. To burnish papers, ensuring that an article realizes its full potential. Burnishing a paper also means ensuring that sufficient information is included in the published article to enable both the validation of results and the replication of the study.

This chapter will explore both of these objectives of peer review and also identify the roles and responsibilities of a peer reviewer and the commonplace expectations various stakeholders in the publication process place on peer review. Very importantly, we will question how the peer reviewers themselves have come to be trusted as appropriately qualified experts in their fields.

PEER REVIEW AS GATEKEEPER

While we are primarily concerned with the modern peer review of journal articles, early scientific research was, in fact, typically communicated in books, in private correspondence, or in periodic scientific/academic meetings.

Observed in retrospect, we can see certain obvious limits to these early forms of scholarly communication in science. The book is best suited either to the publication of years of accumulated research or to the lengthy exposition of grand theories, while private correspondence restricts the distribution of new ideas only to a few recipients. Perhaps we could say that the limited distribution of research results through private correspondence suited early researchers, who might have preferred to restrict discourse to members of their rather exclusive circles; today, however, it is accepted that the journal article is the most appropriate vehicle to publish the results of a single scientific experiment or study.

For the 300 years following the launch of the Royal Society's *Philosophical Transactions* in 1665, scientific journals proliferated around the world, and their formats changed little in that time. Journal publishers generated a huge volume of published material, and this established the scientific journal as the accepted medium by which researchers communicated new ideas and the results of their experiments (Björk).

Yet the development of modern peer review is not, oddly enough, tied directly to the development of these journals. While scientific journals have long assumed the role of guardians of the "official" literature, acting as curators of what could be considered valid research and establishing the standards whereby membership in their exclusive society is granted, the conduct of peer review at these journals has actually evolved considerably. The new forms of peer review reflect the maturity and complexity of various fields of study, the increasing sophistication of research methods, and those recent technological developments, related to the Internet, that allow for various new forms of peer review, such as collaborative review from researchers scattered across the globe who have never met, which would have been inconceivable until quite recently.

The earliest journals were the self-published products of learned societies whose membership comprised various practitioners, clinicians, and subject experts and whose research coalesced around these emerging journals. The notion that these journals required some mechanism of peer assessment and validation was not, however, apparent at first. Authors did not expect their work to be peer-reviewed in the manner to which modern authors are now accustomed, as Albert Einstein's reaction to the external review of his article by *Physical Review* demonstrates, as noted in the previous chapter (Kennefick). These earlier journals typically handled the assessment of a paper "in house," usually by calling on a select group of the members of the society who published a particular journal (Spier).

The advent of peer review in these early journals could be interpreted, in retrospect, as an organic response to the proliferation of articles submitted to them, with journals outsourcing the increasing burden of assessment to external peer reviewers (Burnham). This emerging mechanism of peer review also provided readers with the assurance that what they were reading had been validated, tested, and corrected by fellow experts before it was published. This validation was a welcome benefit, but it was not the sole motivation for developing the modern peer-review process.

Many publications, indeed, continued even until the 1960s to rely on the whim of the designated editor in chief to determine which articles were selected for publication (Fyfe), but nonetheless, it remains clear that the use of experts as peer reviewers had become, by the mid-20th century, the modus operandi by which the scientific communities gathered around particular journals came to vet the flow of research papers. Journals began to use the very same people who either published in or read the journal to collectively validate the results and provide highly technical knowledge in an ever-specializing world.

The system of peer review that emerged in this period was one that allowed scientific and academic output to be granted a stamp of approval while also maintaining an internal, self-regulating, and peer-enabled form of authority. Peer review is precisely a process whereby an author's *peers* were asked, as they still are today, to consider whether they believed that a manuscript deserved to be published, either in its submitted form or following successful revision based on their comments, suggestions, and corrections. This thumbs-up / thumbs-down component of peer review—the acceptance or rejection of a paper—is what we understand to be its *gatekeeper function*. In other words, peers ask whether the research paper under consideration should be allowed to pass through the metaphorical gates (i.e., the threshold for acceptability) barring entry into the corpus of "officially approved" published literature in any given field of study.

At this point, we need to consider a subtle distinction in what we understand the gatekeeper function to mean as applied to two (maybe three, depending on the journal) different stakeholders: the reviewer, the editor in chief, and for those journals that operate such a workflow, an editorial board member / associate editor who can help the editor in chief select reviewers and post a recommendation or decision regarding the worthiness of a paper for publication. Peer reviewers are usually asked whether they would accept, revise (often split in to some variant of minor and major revision), or reject a paper. However, the specific act of *posting a decision* is typically charged to only one person, the editor in chief.

Why? Primarily because the editor in chief oversees the entire publication plan for a journal. Reviewers see only the article they have been asked to review. Editors will also be conscious of economic restraints, such as editorial page budgets. Typically, journals have a limited number of pages they can publish in a given year imposed on them by their publishers. Editors, therefore, must ensure that they do not accept more material than they can publish and do not exceed the budget. As a result, an overextended editor might be compelled to reject an article that in leaner years would have been accepted; a paper does not clear peer review because of quality alone. The editor in chief can also stand up to interference from other agents seeking to influence the direction of the journal through its decision-making processes, such as powerful thought leaders, people with vested financial interests, governments, or those chasing improved impact factors. Conversely, weak editors can be influenced by such individuals. Most obviously, however, along with their editorial boards, editors will have determined the thresholds of acceptability for their journals, the details of which few reviewers would be aware. The difference between editor-based decision making today and in the prewar years is that editors now take into consideration the opinions of peer reviewers rather than acting as the sole arbiter of what is acceptable for publication.

With the dynamic of editorial power in mind, we should acknowledge that peer review is no guarantee of quality, and peer reviewers do not always decide whether a paper should be published. To be accepted for publication in some journals represents the pinnacle of academic achievement, indicated by the journal's demand that the paper provide very high levels of evidence, originality of thinking, or the likelihood of maximal impact on current thought. At the other end of the spectrum, however, some journals are simply looking to fill their page budgets and are content to publish a some-what weak paper. So while reviewers often *think* that they have the power to determine the fate of a manuscript, ultimately, the gatekeeper is still the editor. This can, and frequently does, lead to (sometimes vocal) reviewer disgruntlement when the editor's decision runs counter to the reviewer's judgment.

So what do we mean precisely when we say that the peer-review process provides a gatekeeper function? Whether as reviewers or editors (the latter of whom are almost always practicing researchers and subject experts and not full-time professional editors), expert researchers determine whether a paper deserves to receive the publication's stamp of approval. Publication in the journal can mean different things, but in essence, it should be understood that a paper written by experts has been judged by other experts (review-ers, editors) to be worthy of dissemination to yet more experts (readers). This does not necessarily mean that all parties agreed with the authors or accepted every finding in a paper, but if the results are preliminary and the conclusions are appropriately circumspect, a paper can be accepted for publication even if there is debate about the complete veracity of the ideas presented, the strength of the data collected, or the technique used to con-duct the study.

So what function, precisely, do these gatekeepers perform in the peer-review process? In essence, we should expect that an article published in a peer-reviewed journal has been read by subject experts ahead of publication and that fellow experts have approved the paper for publication and also helped the author(s) correct earlier drafts. We assume all this to be true at any journal that claims to operate peer review, but as we will see later, this gatekeeper process is (potentially) being undermined as trust in the process of scholarly self-regulation—which has become so implicit in the entire foundation of peer review—might slowly be eroding.

How is the gatekeeper function imposed daily at the vast majority of journals? The first step in the process usually involves having the editor (or a member of the editorial team) triage a paper to determine whether it contains any fundamental—presumably unfixable—flaws. The suitability of the article for publication at the journal to which it was submitted is also considered. Once a manuscript passes that initial phase, it makes its way to two or more reviewers. These reviewers have usually been invited to volunteer their time to provide an evaluation. Those sending the invitations to review—if they perform their role properly—will have selected the peer reviewers because their known expertise matches the subject matter of the paper.

Once the manuscript is in the hands of the reviewers, the reviewers use a somewhat standard set of criteria to determine whether they believe a paper should be published. Each journal provides its own unique set of criteria, but commonly used assessment benchmarks include the following:

- *Originality*—are new data or novel concepts presented?
- *Validity*—can the results or claims be tested and reproduced?
- *Context*—are the authors aware of other similar work, most obviously as expressed in the completeness of the references?
- *Claims*—is the tone of the discussion and conclusion in line with the results?
- *Accuracy*—is the paper free of obvious errors?
- *Synthesis*—if the article is a review of previously published work, is it comprehensive, balanced, and clearly built on a carefully designed literature search?
- *Limitations*—do limitations exist and have the authors properly acknowledged them?
- *Techniques*—if applicable, were the appropriate techniques or procedures applied correctly?

- *Ethics*—was the study ethical? Do the authors present any conflicts of interest?
- *Implications*—does the paper advance understanding? What does it contribute to a given field of study? Is it confirmatory (either in a positive or an unhelpful manner)?

Naturally, the application of these criteria can be arbitrarily applied between reviewers and across journals. Editors often, as a consequence, are compelled to seek the opinions of a third reviewer (or fourth or fifth, etc.), as attitudes between reviewers can be highly divergent. Reviewers might even agree on what needs to be corrected with an initial submission but still be split heavily on the fate of the paper. One reviewer's minor revision recommendation is another's rejection.

The job of the editor is to make sense of these reviewer preferences before rendering the final disposition. He or she has to do this while also addressing such different factors as the educational mission of the journal, the desires of the readership, and other critical issues such as ethical legitimacy. This is the conclusive step in the peer-review process, and it is the editors who must determine whether a particular reviewer was "too tough," whether the reviewer was ultimately qualified for the role of assessing a given manuscript, whether the reviewer was able to account for an important methodological issue, or whether a particular reviewer might have evaluated a paper while drawing on (consciously or otherwise) different cultural constructs, personal biases, and other external influences. An editor, for example, must also gauge whether a reviewer's brief review (sadly commonplace) was possibly indicative of having made only a cursory reading of the paper, with scant checking for validity and a general failure to contemplate a manuscript's findings and the implications of those findings.

BURNISHING THE INITIAL SUBMISSION

Assessing and allowing a paper to proceed to publication is only one aspect of peer review. The second major component of peer review is to correct, amend, and polish a paper before it is published. Ideally, the outcome of this burnishing process is that the finished article represents the best paper possible, at least given such constraints as the limits of the study, the ability and resources of the authors, and to some extent, the limits of the journal executing peer review.

Obviously, the best possible scenario involves a paper that describes a well-conducted study and is written up carefully and accurately with methodological particularity. Such papers typically require little more than minor revisions, and one hopes that reviewers will identify these minor problems and note possible amendments in their comments.

Other papers might be based on elegantly executed studies but have been poorly written. Poor writing is quite commonplace and typically entails a failure to describe the study methodology adequately, the questionable use of statistical techniques, or the inadequate referencing of the paper. The research might also be poorly contextualized, which hinders assessment of its significance. Equally, language might be overblown, with evident bias and use of spin. So problems do not lie wholly with grammar, syntax, spelling, the misapplication of terms, or the erroneous use of words by authors writing in their nonnative language; the reality is that authors—with depressing regularity, it seems—simply do not *include* all relevant, pertinent information to allow the reader to assess the validity of the claims a paper makes (Chan and Altman).

An example of this poor writing could be a report of a randomized controlled trial that does not describe how patients were selected. A comprehensive review article might not elaborate on why some literature was discussed, while other articles were excluded. Another example might involve a poorly described (or nonexistent) outline of the origin of an idea or a poor description of a disease condition etiology. This often happens because experts in one niche of a field believe that such information is common knowledge and that description is redundant, but this decision might render papers incomprehensible or open to misinterpretation for other readers. More often, however, researchers are simply not sufficiently skilled in the art of writing a paper and have likely received little to no training on how to write up research for publication. Peer review, in other words, is deployed not only to catch a paper's errors and omissions but also to point out how to correct them. In such instances, as described previously, an article would typically require major revision with requests to rewrite significant portions of the manuscript.

A third type of paper is a poorly conducted study that is, nonetheless, well written, so the reviewers believe that the authors will be able to correct some of the study's defects. It is quite customary in such circumstances for a reviewer to request that the authors repeat their experiments. For an observational study, authors might be asked to consider including more data or reanalyze the original data. Authors are also frequently asked to read additional materials and determine if this new information influences their findings or the new ideas/concepts they are trying to advance. Often extra reading is recommended to help flesh out a reference section that is perhaps rather thin. In most cases, such requests following peer review demand a major revision or even a complete rewrite of the paper if the reviewers and editors believe the paper is salvageable. If, however, the reviewers believe that the problems are insurmountable, the authors are incapable of addressing the problem, or corrective measures might simply take too long, the paper is more likely to be rejected.

The fourth type of paper is typically an inadequate write-up of a weak study or poorly conceived idea. Seasoned editors in any discipline, regardless of the standing of their journals, will attest to the remarkable frequency at which such material is submitted. With the proliferation of submissions to journals in recent years, editors are immediately rejecting some papers even before full peer review in an effort to avoid reviewer burnout (Watkinson). There is, after all, little point in sending out to full peer review an obviously flawed paper that cannot be rescued even with the provision of excellent peer-review comments. In such a scenario, precious reviewer resources would have been wasted on poor papers and perfectly decent papers would not get the reviews they deserve.

Finally, a fifth type of paper might well fit into any of the categories outlined previously, but perhaps the biggest problem is that the paper contributes nothing new. The question of novelty is where peer review can become something of a lottery experience for the authors. Reviewers who are more lenient or perhaps less versed in the subject matter might simply judge the paper on its own internal merits, with no reference to the body of literature into which it would fit. Equally, some reviewers might judge that such a paper is wholly unoriginal and provides no advance to our current understanding, even in the smallest of incremental manners.

So how are papers burnished and polished for publication? How does peer review ensure that papers realize their full potential? How are errors and omissions caught? Peer reviewers are typically asked to post a recommendation regarding publication (usually some variant of accept, reject, and revise), maybe answer a specific question (e.g., does the paper cite all relevant material?), possibly grade some aspect of the paper (e.g., originality, future contribution to the field), and typically provide both confidential remarks to the editors and specific comments to the author. The overwhelming majority of journals utilize online submission systems, all of which offer a basic template to capture the information delineated previously. Some journals go one step further and will offer detailed instructions on how they would like the respective comments to the editor and author to be ordered. Rather frustratingly, many editors will attest to reviewers simply blowing through these instructions and writing what they feel is important, which can lead to a huge disparity in the usefulness of any comments provided.

Remarks directed to the editor are intended to provide a summary explanation of the reviewer's grade for a paper and a context for the reviewer's opinions (such as his or her own experiences). On occasion, these comments can also discreetly raise issues such as ethical concerns (e.g., questioning whether the authors received Institutional Review Board approval for their study). Along with such observations, the reviewer can also assess whether he or she believes the authors will be able to revise their paper. With unfettered freedom to express opinions, the comments to editors can reveal genuine concerns that a reviewer might feel uncomfortable expressing directly to the authors for various reasons. Additionally, and intriguingly, confidential comments to the editor can sometimes reveal interdisciplinary politics, bias, and gossip, all of which means that the decision-making process does not necessarily exist in a vacuum. The confidential comments can also act as a confessional whereby reviewers can disclose their own limitations that might somewhat impinge on their abilities to fully judge a paper, such as a lack of knowledge on a specific point.

Beyond opinion, ideally the reviewer's comments for editors should also include a brief, noneditorialized summary of the paper and the reviewer's interpretation of the intended objectives and outcomes of the paper. The reviewer's factual account can reveal to the editor both the potential and the limits of a paper, but it can also disclose whether the reviewer truly understood it.

Comments to the authors are normally the central element of article peer review. These remarks are intended to help authors improve their papers, and in this context, reviewers are not supposed to pass judgment on the suitability of a paper for publication. Unfortunately, peer review can be horribly uneven. This might be due to the amount of time a reviewer gives to the assessment of the paper or his or her own true level of understanding of a topic. Consequently, remarks from reviewers range from simple statements such as "This is a nice paper that contributes to the field" to lengthy, elegantly espoused observations that provide crucial support to an author who is revising his or her paper. Obviously the latter scenario is preferred for many reasons, not least because for authors operating without collaborators or a consultative support structure at their institution, good peer review can actually deliver a vital form of mentorship. In a reviewing system in which there is little to no uniformity in approach or training in the art of peer review, however, the comments can be delivered and interpreted in a manner ranging from the antagonistic to the collegial. Ultimately, the aim is to improve the completeness of reporting, enhance the presentation of information, offer alternative perspectives, and even provide advice to authors to help them better understand their own work.

Ideally, reviewer comments to the author should begin with a summary statement of what the paper aims to achieve and state whether the reviewer believes the authors have succeeded in achieving those goals. Furthermore, a well-constructed reviewer summary should also highlight the major findings, strengths, and significance of a manuscript as well as deficiencies. Such a summary is actually quite essential, as many authors do not quite understand the larger significance of their work and the reviewer's comments can help them moderate their language and style of presentation.

Having presented a summary of the paper, the best reviewer will then break a paper down section by section, commenting on the methods, results, discussion, and conclusion and also ideally differentiating between what he or she regards as major and minor issues. Comments are usually posed as short and impactful questions, suggestions, or corrections that allow the authors to clearly determine what they need to amend. The expectation is that when authors revise their papers as directed by the reviewer comments in response to the initial manuscript submission, they must also provide a detailed, point-by-point response to the reviewer comments—hence the need for reviewers to clearly and succinctly outline each individual point that requires clarification, correction, or revision.

So what are some of the common critiques that help authors polish a paper? The list of effective comments to authors that follows, though not exhaustive, provides some of the essential elements of a good review. In other words, a well-constructed peer review that is evaluating a trial, literature review, or study would ideally address these issues and provide authors with the feedback they need to amend their papers accordingly. For medical and scientific journals, articles usually are formatted along the lines of the commonly used introduction, methods, results, and discussion (IMRAD) structure, which provides the organization of the well-constructed peer review. Specific fields, and certainly individual journals, typically provide a set of directions to reviewers to ensure that they address certain elements unique to their fields as they consider a paper.

Common components of effective comments to authors include the following:

Methods
- Did the authors adequately report what they did?
- Are descriptive statistics adequately reported?
- How many subjects are in the analysis?
- Is there a potential for bias or missing data?
- Is the sample selection and size appropriate for the conclusions drawn?
- Is the experimental procedure carefully described?
- Is the context for data collection described in detail?
- Are the inclusion or exclusion criteria for objects of study (patients, phenomena, previously published literature, etc.) effectively outlined?
- Can the research question be answered with the study design used?
- Does the paper provide an outcome assessment with unconventional or nonvalidated measures?

Results

- Do the results answer the research question asked? Do the authors try to make inferences from the results for which the data, and its collection, were not designed?
- Are the results presented properly and in a comprehensible manner?
- Are tables and figures used effectively? Are all images of a high enough resolution to interpret?
- What are the primary and secondary outcomes from this study?
- Are the results credible? What evidence, as a reviewer, can you use to validate your response to that question?

Discussion

- Does the data presented support the conclusions or contentions the authors make?
- How are the data analyzed? Do the authors indicate which variables were analyzed by which tests, error control strategy, rationale for choice of tests, and missing data strategy?
- Does the discussion section include a substantial discussion of limitations?
- Are the results related to earlier studies to provide context and comparisons?
- Does the discussion section successfully navigate from the specific (the study under review) to the general (current understanding) as a way to provide context?

Conclusions

- Are any study limitations appropriately addressed?
- Are pointers directing possible future research endeavors provided?

General Observations

- Do the authors demonstrate familiarity with the subject, concept, technique, or principle?
- Is the reference section complete and up to date? Within any review of the previous literature, did the authors explain why they included/ excluded certain articles?

- Is a study underpowered? Is there an adequately sized data set or sample size to draw conclusions with confidence?
- Is there enough information in the article to reproduce the experiment/study/trial?
- Is the work currently under review too similar to work previously published by the author(s)? What new content/data does the paper under review present?
- After reading the paper, ask yourself, "So what?" If the answer is hard to discern, consider whether the paper is deserving of publication.
- Did the authors adhere to the reporting criteria outlined in the appropriate reporting guideline (e.g., CONSORT for randomized controlled trials; STROBE for observational studies)?
- Where relevant, does the paper under review adhere to current diagnostic conventions?
- For revised submissions, have the authors made a "good faith effort" to address the critiques of reviewers and editorial staff of the initially submitted version of the paper?
- Would any other experiments or additional information improve the paper? How much better would the paper be if this extra work was done, and how difficult would such work be to do or provide?
- Does the paper require reorganization to flow better and add clarity to the message the author intends to impart?
- Does the paper require edits for language?

WHO IS THE PEER IN PEER REVIEW?

Many journals, especially the most established titles, will typically retain a list of "go-to" reviewers, expanding that pool as new experts emerge or through suggestions either from reviewers who declined the invitation to review or from authors themselves (resulting in a potentially alarming conflict of interest). Once again, if those selecting potential reviewers are doing their jobs properly, the reviewers will have been adequately screened before they are asked to conduct a review.

Criteria for selecting a reviewer vary by journal, but these criteria typically include a sense of the reviewer's demonstrated level of knowledge in a particular subject (e.g., published papers, grants awarded, lectures given, being a thought leader in the field), a track record of writing full and fair reviews, an association with a known and experienced contributor to the field if the potential reviewer is an early career researcher, and crucially, no conflicts of interest, such as an obvious vested financial interest in the results, a personal/professional connection to the authors, a standing in competitive relation to the authors, or an instance where the reviewer's work is being challenged by the paper under review.

Are all reviewers *suitably qualified* to determine the fate of a paper? Are all researchers naturally potential reviewers? No and no, quite simply. The reality is, however, that while all journals should vet a proposed reviewer thoroughly before allowing him or her to critique a paper, most journals—beyond a select few—are underresourced and under incredible pressure to provide rapid initial decisions. The result of this pressure is that some of these journals are, frankly, unconcerned by who reviews a paper and satisfied to secure anyone whose name can be retained in their submission and review system.

Considering these limitations, it is not surprising that journals often restrict their choice of reviewers to friends and acquaintances. When those familiar individuals turn down the opportunity to review, journals then cast their nets far and wide to capture a willing reviewer. Obviously, the potential of introducing error and inefficiency into the peer-review process increases the further the reviewer is from a journal's usual orbit. This tendency for a journal to rely on friends and acquaintances to critique papers naturally begs the question as to what—or *who*—constitutes the "peer" in peer review.

Unfortunately, it is a fact that the journal editors and thought leaders in a particular area of study might not fully understand what makes a suitable reviewer. Visible leaders in any given field are not always expert reviewers—they might be more skilled as politicians or organizers, in fact, and might not even be stellar individual researchers, having really only collaborated alongside others who have actually driven major research projects forward. Other individuals might be quite brilliant clinicians or practitioners, and thus their opinions are obviously needed, but they might not be equally adept at spotting methodological flaws in a paper or the incorrect or inappropriate application of a statistical technique. The notion of being a suitably qualified reviewer also stretches to the aforementioned concerns about conflicts of interest or potential bias. As few reviewers ever embody the "perfect fit" for a paper under consideration, journals should ideally seek to have reviewers with a blend of backgrounds, interests, and capabilities on hand to ensure that a balanced perspective can be achieved.

In most scientific and academic fields, individuals become recognized as experts, practitioners, or competent exponents by *qualifying* following a course of study. However, there is currently no formal mechanism of qualification to become a peer reviewer. Indeed, though some journals, learned societies, and publishers offer reviewer training, most instruction on assessing a paper is mentor driven at best and nonexistent at worst. Many reviewers simply learn on the job, absorbing the directives of the various journals they work for or witnessing the comments of the other reviewers for a particular paper. When functioning as reviewers, regular authors can draw on their experiences as recipients of critiques of their own work, recalling what comments were especially insightful.

As a result of this lack of requisite reviewer training, there is really no set of reviewer core competencies to which a journal must refer. Such competencies would likely consist of some level of methodological grounding, an understanding of how to break down a paper, and critically, how to write up a review in an effective manner. As we will discuss elsewhere in this book, there is concern that there is more to being a reviewer than being a subject expert, and this has obvious implications for our confidence in the veracity and quality of the material that is published in peer-reviewed journals.

Journals with sufficient resources can plug such gaps in the knowledge or experience of reviewers by using reviewers—sometimes even one individual—who are specialists in particular statistical or methodological areas. A statistical consultant, for example, is normally retained to examine the statistical design outlined in a paper rather than to assess the scientific content. He or she will provide feedback on the accuracy of the statistics presented, the appropriateness of the statistical technique used, and the correct application of a technique. The specialist will likely also assess the analytical plan. A methodology expert, on the other hand, might be employed to assess the application of the research method as well as the completeness of methodological reporting. The methodology expert will often perform specialist evaluations for specific article types. For instance, for retrospective studies, he or she might check to see if data are being used in ways that conflict with the design of the original collection. These experts will also concern themselves with issues related to the presentation of results.

Such specialist reviewers are typically used as complements to subject experts, but they can make or break a paper, especially in the detection of flaws or in discerning the overstatement of the significance of results. Depending on the journal, specialist reviewers can be deployed at different points in the peer-review process. For instance, the *Journal of Sexual Medicine* enacts a methodological triage before the manuscript is seen by the editors in an effort to weed out weak papers. Others, such as *Headache: The Journal of Head and Face Pain*, deploy the statistical or methodological consultant as an additional reviewer. When resources are precious, the specialist might perhaps only be called on to review papers that have favorably completed peer assessment ahead of a decision from the editor.

ROLES AND RESPONSIBILITIES OF PEER REVIEWERS

Any form of self-regulation is predicated on trust in the people and the process they support, and we can say with some confidence that a lack of transparency and confidence in the peer-review process is ultimately harmful to all participants in the practices of research and publication. Yet in the absence of any formal training, many reviewers are simply unaware of their responsibilities and barely understand what they have been asked to do.

What should we be able to expect from reviewers? First and foremost, reviewers must supply a comprehensive, timely, and carefully balanced review to an author whose effort and trust in the system must be respected. Authors submit papers to journals in good faith and trust that editors and reviewers will treat their work with respect, will maintain the confidentiality of the submission, will not appropriate their ideas or data, and will not cause damaging delays—intentionally or otherwise. Authors should be able to expect a level of courtesy from a journal, confident that they will not be insulted or undermined or, in the worst of cases, have their character challenged.

Reviewers also have a second core responsibility: they must understand their own strengths and limitations, declining the opportunity to review if they are not thoroughly qualified. Reviewers obviously have a responsibility to protect the sanctity of a field's body of literature by ensuring that only the most deserving of papers are published. A reviewer's failure to perform his or her role allows weak papers to infiltrate the literature, muddying what can be discerned as valuable, validated, trusted, and reliable work. A failure to review work in sufficient depth can also contribute to a very real sense of waste when weak papers are published, potentially leading to misdirected future research, wasted research funds, and wasted effort reviewing and publishing material that did not deserve to be published (Macleod et al.).

In a sense, reviewers—especially if they are also authors—have a responsibility to "pay it forward," or to return the favor to other participants in the system of scholarly communication. This systemic quid pro quo is referred to in an editorial in *Nature Neuroscience* (2009) as a "civic duty" for authors ("Striving for Excellence"). For peer review to survive, authors too should dedicate time to evaluate papers as others have volunteered time and expertise to assess their papers. Indeed, most reviewers feel there is a benefit to doing that: 91 percent of respondents to a 2008 survey indicated that the reason they perform peer review was to "play [their] part as a member of the academic community" (Ware). Though peer review is a voluntary endeavor in all but a few cases, that fact alone does not absolve reviewers from the responsibility to participate.

Other than issues of timeliness (authors are much less patient than reviewers and editors), there does seem to be a match between what authors expect from peer review and what reviewers aim to deliver: full and balanced assessment, polite critique, refinement of the presentation of results and ideas, the handling of the paper in confidence, and ensuring that expertise is effectively directed at improving the paper. Despite much grumbling and some recent tinkering with its delivery and openness, the durability of peer review speaks to its ultimate effectiveness and the overall satisfaction of all stakeholders in the process.

CHALLENGES OF
PEER REVIEW

Peer review has become ubiquitous in scholarly journals, being seen as the hallmark of a journal's credibility and what qualifies research as science. Yet, as we have seen, peer review did not originate as the guarantor of the validity of research, and it is clear that it has not always performed that function effectively. For example, a study was conducted at the *British Medical Journal* (*BMJ*), taking a paper that was about to be published and introducing eight errors. The paper was then sent out to 420 potential reviewers, 221 of whom responded. None of the respondents spotted more than five of the errors; the average respondent identified only two errors; and 16 percent didn't identify any errors at all (Godlee, Gale, and Martyn). However, it is unclear how many of the reviewers continued to review the paper after spotting the first two or three errors.

A similar conclusion is demonstrated looking at published papers. García-Berthou and Alcaraz (2004) found statistical inconsistencies in 38 percent of papers in *Nature* and 25 percent in the *BMJ*. The number of papers retracted every year for problems in methodology, for breaches of research ethics, or for fabrication of data is indicative of the fact that peer review does not, and cannot, be a truth sieve through which only valid science can pass (see http://www.retractionwatch.com/). John Ioannidis (2005) presented a probability algorithm to demonstrate the likelihood that most published studies are false. As well as methodological problems, factors such as conflicts of interests, prejudice, and perceptions concerning what are the "hotter" topics have served as ineffective filters for journals. These are problems of editorial peer review that, among other things, increase the likelihood that a journal will publish articles with false conclusions. If we accept that the majority of published work is incorrect and that the primary purpose of peer review is to prevent the publication of false and invalid research, then it is clear why many now question the system of traditional peer review.

One can say that peer review does serve a useful function in the filtering of submissions, citing research into the fate of rejected articles. Fifty to sixty-five percent of articles rejected from the *Annals of Internal Medicine* were published elsewhere, indicating that as many as 50 percent of submissions were simply unpublishable and rightly kept out of the scientific literature (Williamson).

If we were to set the standard lower and say that we expect peer review to improve the quality of papers, then the results are less clear. A study published in the *Journal of the American Medical Association* (*JAMA*) would seem to bear this out, concluding that "editorial peer review, although widely used, is largely untested and its effects are uncertain" (Jefferson et al., "Effects"). Similarly, a Cochrane review (2003, updated in 2007) of studies into peer review found "little empirical evidence to support the use of editorial peer review as a mechanism to ensure quality of biomedical research, despite its widespread use and costs" (also see Hopewell et al.).

However, the absence of study data about the effects of peer review is not the same as evidence that peer review has a null effect. Surveys of researchers consistently find that peer review is perceived as improving the quality of papers. A survey of 4,000 people conducted by Sense about Science found that 9 out of 10 authors believe that peer review improved their last published paper (Mulligan, Hall, and Raphael). This is the same proportion reported by a similar survey of 3,040 academics conducted by the Publishing Research Consortium (Ware; also see Lu). In the perception of authors and reviewers, the question is not whether peer review improves the quality of papers but to what extent and in what areas. In descending order, Ware (2008) found that authors perceived some improvement in presentation (94 percent), language or readability (86 percent), missing or inaccurate references (78 percent), scientific errors (64 percent), and statistical errors (55 percent). These opinions indicate that peer review does improve (or at least is perceived to improve) the quality of papers but is less significant in those areas that might be considered most integral—that is, questions of validity.

The effectiveness of peer review is also challenged by the fact that reviewers are not often unanimous in their recommendations. Rothwell (2000) found that the probability of two reviewers agreeing were only slightly better than chance. While using two to three independent reviewers is usually considered the standard for peer review, Rothwell concluded that you would need six reviewers per paper to produce a reliable result. Those journals that operate with only a single reviewer per paper—and there are plenty of such journals—are particularly vulnerable to the inconsistency in peer judgment. This discrepancy occurs not only in the general recommendation but in the specific requests for revisions. Those authors unfortunate enough to have new reviewers look at a manuscript they have revised can sometimes find themselves being requested to add in elements that the previous reviewers asked them to remove (or vice versa).

In addition to inconsistency, there are other perceived problems with peer review, including the speed of the process, financial cost, potential bias, instances of abuse, and difficulty of detecting fraud or misconduct (Williamson).

The speed of peer review, and thus the speed of publication, is often a surprise for the uninitiated. The fact is that peer review is conducted unpaid by academics or practitioners who have other, more rewarding, calls on their time: "A single peer review takes about four hours, but organizing two or three reviews takes on average four months or more" (Johnston). In the fast-paced area of medicine, for instance, waiting a quarter of a year or more for a first decision delays dissemination of significant, sometimes life-changing, results. While there are tools and techniques for reducing unnecessary delays, improving the speed of peer review will be difficult while it depends on reviewers donating their spare time.

The cost of peer review is a significant concern, especially for publishers in an age of limited growth in subscriptions and disruption to the market from open access and other forms of digital dissemination. The cost of the editorial process is between $90 and $600 per article, far more costly than copyediting or printing or other publishing services (Williamson). This cost is incurred even though reviewers are not paid; it includes editor honoraria, fees for electronic systems, and the salaries of editorial office staff, among other things. Were reviewers to be paid, it is unlikely that they would ever be paid equivalent to the time they devote to peer review, and in most cases, such reviewer payments would prove prohibitive to continued publication. Those journals that do pay reviewers often cover the costs by charging a submission fee.

Bias in peer review is more difficult to evaluate. Williamson (2003), for example, asserts that there is evidence of prestige bias, geographical bias, and gender bias. Other common concerns about peer review are the danger of confirmation bias (the tendency to read evidence as confirming your own preconceptions) and the conservatism of peer review, favoring consensus over proposals from outside the current paradigms. However, in a wide-ranging review examining such studies, Lee et al. (2012) questioned Williamson's methodological assumptions and found little empirical evidence for these concerns about bias. Anecdotal evidence does indicate that bias and prejudice occurs, though it is difficult to determine how widespread it is and what impact it has on publication.

It is well known that peer review can be open to abuse. One common problem is that the line between authors and reviewers can actually become blurred. Some have encountered cases where a supervisor of the lead author was initially recommended as reviewer of a paper only to later claim to also be an author on the same paper. There have been other cases where reviewers (or even editors) have attempted to gain authorship credit on a paper by offering to collaborate with authors for a revised version. This problem of "gift authorship" can be preempted by adopting clear policies about what qualifies one as an author, but the incentive of an easy publication means that this form of abuse will always be a danger.

More recently, so-called peer review rings have emerged, where authors have created fabricated reviewer accounts that allowed them to subvert and manipulate the peer-review process. Hundreds of published articles were retracted after it became apparent that authors reviewed their own work or had a friendly third-party review done on their behalf (Oransky).

Other recorded forms of abuse would leave the casual observer incredulous, ranging from attempts by reviewers to plagiarize studies they review, "scooping" the original authors by rapidly publishing or releasing their data in a public forum such as an academic conference, and even giving authors the option to recommend reviewers (many journals struggle to find reviewers, which is why they sometimes ask authors for help—the potential for abuse is obvious, though). There are now agencies that offer to create fake e-mail accounts for unscrupulous authors to use for their recommended reviewers so that, if selected, these accounts can provide favorable reviews and increase the chances of publication. This problem highlights an overdependence on recommended reviewers by editors, who often struggle to get reviewers to agree, as well as an overdependence by editors on the recommendations of reviewers in preference to their own assessments of a paper.

In noting that reviewers are "almost useless" at spotting fraud or misconduct, Williamson is really only highlighting the fact that reviewers are limited by circumstance. Reviewers were not present when a research study was conducted, when the results were analyzed, or when the conclusions were authored. Often the only information the reviewer will have is the submitted paper. If the authors have misreported their methodology, omitted reference to their unethical conduct, or fabricated their data, how would the reviewer be able to tell? Sometimes a reviewer might be able to identify that the reported results look "fishy" or too good to be true, but accusations of misconduct would be hugely detrimental to a researcher's career, and reviewers are unlikely to bandy such accusations lightly. To address this concern, efforts such as the Enhancing the Quality and Transparency of Health Research (EQUATOR) Network have emerged. The EQUATOR Network is an international initiative that promotes transparent and accurate reporting and wider use of robust reporting guidelines. Currently they provide information on more than 300 guidelines (http://www.equator-network.org).

A reviewer might spot other types of fabrication, such as image manipulation. But most lack the training and expertise to identify all possible forms of manipulation. Similarly, a reviewer can only spot plagiarized material if he or she happens to have read and remembered the prior publication. While reviewers can assist in spotting cases of misconduct, it is simply unrealistic to expect reviewers to identify such misconduct consistently (let alone infallibly).

Another threat to the peer-review system is the advent of "predatory" open-access publishers. These are sham journals that exist only to take advantage of the author-pays business model by publishing almost anything for a price. Most of these fake publications claim to conduct peer review but in fact do not. Young researchers from developing countries are particularly at risk of becoming the victim of predatory publications (Xia). Awareness of predatory open-access publishers has grown due the work of Jeffrey Beall, a librarian at the University of Colorado Denver, as well as some high-profile exposés. In 2010, Beall coined the term "predatory publisher" and created what has come to be known as "Beall's List of potential, possible, or probable predatory scholarly open-access publishers" (Butler). In 2009, Phil Davis, a Cornell University doctoral student interested in investigating the increasing prevalence of scam journals, submitted a manuscript composed of computer-generated nonsense to a suspected predatory journal (Basken). The paper was accepted and the ruse exposed on the popular industry blog the *Scholarly Kitchen*. More recently, John Bohannon, a staff writer for *Science* magazine, targeted the open-access system in 2013 by submitting an intentionally deeply flawed paper to more than 300 open-access journals. Approximately 60 percent of those journals accepted the fake medical paper (Bohannon).

While some have tried to use the practices of predatory publishers to paint all open-access journals and all forms of peer review as illegitimate, it is important to note that most open-access journals are authentic and do carry out peer review in an effort to publish material that contributes to the body of scientific knowledge.

DIFFERENT PERSPECTIVES ON PEER REVIEW

This process of sending manuscripts to independent experts for critical appraisal—peer review—has become a mainstay of academic publishing. Yet despite the perception that peer review is an essential minimum requirement for a journal, and despite general expectations that peer review will be fair to authors and ensure or improve the quality of papers, there is actually considerable variance in the way peer review operates.

According to the Committee on Publication Ethics (COPE), journal editors should make decisions based on importance, originality, clarity, validity, and relevance. Editors should ensure that peer review is fair, unbiased, and timely and that materials submitted are kept confidential while under review. They should also encourage reviewers to comment on ethics, including research misconduct and plagiarism. However, as to the specifics of peer review, COPE states that editors should adopt "peer review methods best suited for their journal and the research community it serves" (Committee on Publication Ethics 6).

According to the International Committee of Medical Journal Editors (ICMJE), journal editors should ensure that manuscripts are reviewed in a timely manner, that reviewers are not part of the editorial staff, and that peer review is "unbiased, independent, and critical." The ICMJE also states, "A peer-reviewed journal is under no obligation to send submitted manuscripts for review, and under no obligation to follow reviewer recommendations, favorable or negative. The editor of a journal is ultimately responsible for the selection of all its content, and editorial decisions might be informed by issues unrelated to the quality of a manuscript, such as suitability for the journal. An editor can reject any article at any time before publication, including after acceptance if concerns arise about the integrity of the work."

Again the ICMJE does not provide stipulations as to the specifics of peer review, recognizing that these will vary among fields and among journals. For this reason, they encourage journals to publish a description of their peer-review process (http://www.icmje.org/).

When considering editorial peer review across all disciplines and subject areas, there is indeed a great deal of difference in practice and process. Some examples are as follows:

> *Number of Reviewers.* There is some intuitive appeal in the idea that more than one reviewer should be consulted to ensure the objectivity of the outcome. While many journals, perhaps the majority, usually require two reviews before making a decision, there are a significant proportion of journals that obtain only one review per manuscript. On the other hand, a significant number of journals require three reviews, or even more, as standard. As cited previously, Rothwell's study indicates that six reviewers would be required to ensure a reliable majority agreement between reviewers, so there is no empirical basis for the preference for two reviewers. Two is probably the preferred standard simply because of the difficulty of acquiring more than two reviews in a timely manner.

Decisions without Review. Many authors now expect that their papers will be sent out for review because there is a general perception that this independent assessment is essential for a fair judgment of their manuscript. However, as quoted previously, the ICMJE (among others) places no requirement on editors to actually send papers out for review. Many journals operate a form of triage, called desk rejects, which dismisses a proportion of papers on submission. For some journals, desk rejects are limited to such reasons as being outside the scope of the journal, but for others, the editors are making an assessment about whether the paper will weather peer review or will definitely be rejected. This triage policy reduces the time authors wait to receive a negative decision, allowing them to submit to another journal more quickly and reducing the number of papers that reviewers need to be found for. However, the fact that not all papers are peer-reviewed and there is no unanimity about those circumstances under which a paper is not sent for review is indicative of the fact that it is editors, not reviewers, who are ultimately responsible for what is published.

Focus of Review. The perception that peer review is the standard for what is worthy to be published assumes that the focus of review is on validity and quality. While most, if not all, journals will ask reviewers to consider these issues, they are not the only factors on which reviewers might be asked to comment. Since many journals are only interested in publishing articles that will be highly cited (to improve their impact factor) or highly downloaded, reviewers might be asked to comment on the novelty or significance of a topic. Since many journals have constraints about page budgets, reviewers might be asked to comment on whether a paper is a high priority for publication. These other decision factors are symptomatic of the fact that journal publishing is not only concerned with maintaining the scientific record.

Objects of Review. While there is probably a general sense among journals as to what peer review entails, there is considerable variance as to what reviewers are expected to comment on. Expectations might include appropriateness of title, succinctness of abstract, relevance of images, quality of language and expression, appropriateness of methodology, validity of statistical analysis, and validity of conclusions, among many other things. Some journals give reviewers specific instructions, perhaps even a checklist or questionnaire detailing those areas to consider, but there are generally few checks and balances to ensure that reviewers actually conduct the review systematically and thoroughly. There is certainly no universally recognized standard as to what reviewers should (and should not) comment on.

Therefore, despite the perception that peer review is the minimum standard for journal publishing and should be a guarantee of the validity of what is published, in reality, peer review as it operates today is a somewhat amorphous and inconsistent practice. Yet this should be of no surprise given how peer review arose and developed. Editors turned to reviewers to supplement their opinions and to assist them in their task of filtering submissions for publication (Spier). Peer review was not established to remove responsibility for decisions from the editor or to act as the guardian of science or a safeguard against unethical or fraudulent papers. Peer review has never been a monolithic concept or standard. This diversity of practice is likely to increase.

TYPES OF PEER REVIEW

For a number of decades, peer review generally operated with either one of two main models: single blind or double blind. Though there were variations of approach, almost all peer-reviewed journals could be classified in this way. However, since the late 1990s, a plethora of alternatives to the traditional models have emerged. The various kinds of peer review now available do not fit neatly into discrete categories, as the types might differ in only one aspect (or in many).

The question of anonymity in peer review, for instance, differs across models. Under single-blind review, the identities of the reviewers are kept secret from the authors; under double-blind review, the identities of the authors are also kept secret from the reviewers. There is also triple-blind review, though this is rarer, where the identities of the authors are kept secret from the editors. Opposing these blind forms of peer review is open peer review, where the identities of the reviewers are revealed to the authors. Open peer review might then be extended to the publication of the reviewers' names as well as the content of their reviews alongside the final article.

Another aspect of peer review is whether it should operate discretely for each journal or whether reviews can be transferred between journals to accelerate the review process and reduce redundancy. A third aspect is whether reviewers operate separately from each other and from the authors or whether the process should be more collaborative. Finally, there is the question of whether peer review should be conducted prior to publication or whether there is a role for postpublication review, either in addition to or instead of prepublication review.

One of the unexplained phenomena related to the development of peer review is the split between single- and double-blind review across subject areas. For example, across Wiley journals, 95 percent of physical science and health science journals operate single-blind peer review, 72 percent of life sciences journals are single blind, but only 15 percent of social sciences and humanities journals. Social sciences and humanities journals are also the only subject category employing triple-blind review (1 percent). There seems no obvious factor or factors that should lead to a preference for author anonymity in these subject areas. Indeed, one might argue that author anonymity would be more important in fields where the potential incentives for bias were more numerous, such as for medical journals. The Wiley statistics also indicate that although the world is changing, it is changing slowly. Of their 1,593 journals, only 8 now offer some form of open peer review and only 4 others offer collaborative review. Single and double blind remain the dominant paradigms for peer review.

ANONYMITY OF REVIEWERS (SINGLE BLIND VERSUS OPEN)

The most common form of peer review, particularly among science journals, is single-blind review. This seems to have been the model of peer review widely adopted when peer review itself became commonplace, and this preference has not radically changed. Under single-blind review, the author does not know who the reviewer is. The key benefit of the anonymity is that it protects reviewers from criticism or the displeasure of authors and thus encourages reviewers to be candid in their evaluation of the manuscript without fear of reprisal. Those who have worked for journals will have experienced the occasional disgruntled author, whether this is a reactionary outburst that can be ignored or a more measured and/or persistent objection that might turn into a formal appeal. In either case, the reviewers are protected from becoming embroiled in this follow-up due to their anonymity.

It is not only the spontaneous form of unpleasantness from which the reviewers are protected. Peer review, as generally operated, is a process that happens in confidence and under the auspices of a specific journal. Reviewers might review several versions of the same paper, but their involvement with the paper is still limited by the requirements of the journal. However, revealing the identities of the reviewers exposes them to the potential for an open-ended and ongoing discussion with the authors outside the auspices of the journal. This is a particular concern for journals working in small fields where powerful personalities can wield excessive influence. While some reviewers might feel comfortable with this open collaboration with authors, others are likely to want some limitation on their commitments. Anonymity protects reviewers from any temptation among authors to contact the reviewers outside the confines of the formal review process.

The major criticism of blinded (or closed) review, however, is that the anonymity offered to reviewers limits their accountability for the recommendations they make, which might determine whether a paper is rejected. Given the importance of being published for career development and for securing research funding, reviewers have a significant position of responsibility. Richard Smith, former editor of the *British Medical Journal* (*BMJ*), writes, "The primary argument against closed peer review is that it seems wrong for somebody making an important judgment on the work of others to do so in secret. A court with an unidentified judge makes us think immediately of totalitarian states and the world of Franz Kafka" (Smith, "Opening").

However, this desire to make reviewers accountable might be misguided. After all, reviewers are already accountable to the editors they serve; they are unlikely to be used for future reviews if their comments are unhelpful or derogatory. In contrast, what sort of accountability is it that opens up reviewers to possible blowback from authors without any mediation or regulation? Also the court analogy is unjustified because authors are free to choose where they submit and are free to publish elsewhere if rejected ("Striving for Excellence"). Comparing reviewers to judges misses the fact that it is the editor who is ultimately responsible for what is published, and the identity of the editor is always known; reviewers are not judge and jury but more akin to expert witnesses. This is not to say that accountability in journal publishing is not important. It is good practice for journals to have an appeal process for investigating complaints from authors, particularly if there are accusations of misconduct by editors or reviewers. However, such processes will only be improved by the increased adoption of ethical standards across journals, not by exposing reviewers.

The ideological impulse toward transparency is not the only motivation for open peer review. When *Nursing Research* adopted a policy of publishing reviewer reports, the reason was not primarily ethical; they wanted to provide instruction to new authors on the workings of the editorial office. By publishing the full paper trail, authors could see how manuscripts are revised and how decisions were made (Dougherty). This kind of guidance is important for new authors; however, it does not seem to require the naming of reviewers or even the publication of real reviews. Illustrative examples, alongside the author guidelines, would serve the same purpose.

Another claimed benefit of open peer review is that it allows reviewers to take credit for their work (Groves). However, it is not evident that reviewers are seeking this kind of credit. According to a survey, the primary reasons for reviewing were duty to the academic community (91 percent agree) and the joy of improving the paper (78 percent agree). In contrast, reviewers were less likely to review if their name was published with the article (38 percent) and if their signed report was published (47 percent; Ware 8–9). Moreover, the benefits that might accrue from being identified as a reviewer on a paper are limited because they will only be apparent to the readers of that paper. If reviewers do want credit, then it is credit that they can use as evidence of their academic activities and thus further their career, such as Continuing Medical Education (CME) credit (for those working in medicine). Publons, a new initiative that aims to give reviewers credit for their reviewing activity, is not predicated on open peer review, though it does facilitate the publication of reviews (https://publons.com). In addition, ORCID, Faculty of 1000, and the Consortia Advancing Standards in Research Administration Information (CASRAI) initiated a community working group to address this question in an effort to develop a standard for reviewer recognition using ORCID identifiers (Padula).

The other main motivation for open peer review is the intuition that it might improve the quality of reviews if reviewers are required to provide their names. However, evidence from trials has not substantiated this intuition. In two trials, open peer review produced no statistically significant increase in quality compared to blinded (van Rooyen 25; Walsh 49). In the third study, blinded reviews received a higher average rating (+ 0.41; 8 percent) than unblinded reviewers. More significant was the increased proportion of reviews rated excellent among the blinded reviews (McNutt 1375). Anecdotally, it was noted that, on balance, open reviews were more courteous and less abusive, but since only a small minority of reviews are abusive, this was not considered to be a significant result (Walsh 48–49; McNutt 1374). Furthermore, though it does seem possible in theory that reviewers might be more motivated to provide lengthier reviews if their names are attached to them, it does not follow that the reviews will be better, primarily because so many reviewers have never received adequate (or indeed any) training on how to conduct good peer review, an issue discussed elsewhere in this book.

On the other hand, there are several problems with open peer review. Some commentators have noted the potential for junior reviewers to have their careers hindered by criticizing more senior colleagues (Walsh 50; "Striving for Excellence"). Others point to potential for damage to working or personal relationships, particularly in a small field: "I do not particularly want the author to know that I was the reviewer who pointed out the boneheaded thing he or she did" (Albanese). There is also potential for nepotism if named reviewers attempt to curry favor with senior colleagues by praising their work in review.

There are added potential problems if reviewers are named and their reviews published, as any published statement is subject to libel law. Any statement made in a review that might be considered defamatory against the author could potentially be the subject of legal action against the reviewer.

The other problem with open peer review is the potential for loss of reviewers. Ware (2008) found that reviewers were less likely to review if their names were published, and trials of peer review found that a number of reviewers will decline to participate in an open review system (Walsh; van Rooyen; Khan). Given that editors often struggle to secure reviewers, the concern about losing reviewers will certainly make editors reluctant to switch to open review unless reviewers' attitudes change.

ANONYMITY OF AUTHORS (DOUBLE BLIND)

The most common form of peer review among social science and humanities journals is double-blind review, where the identities of the authors are kept from the reviewers and vice versa. Though double blind is not widely practiced among science journals, double-blind review has been found to be the preferred model of a majority of respondents (56 percent), and most considered it to be effective (71 percent; Ware 18).

The principle reason for operating double-blind review is to remove the possibility of bias from the review process, so that papers are judged on their merits and not on gender, nationality, status, or other factors related to the author. There is some anecdotal evidence, and some high-profile cases, that indicates that bias does occur, but it is difficult to judge how common bias actually is. Lee et al. (2012) judged that the evidence was inconclusive as to whether double-blind peer review actually reduces bias (11). This might seem counterintuitive—surely anonymity would eliminate any possibility of bias?—but the explanation might be that in order for double-blind review to reduce bias, we would first have to assume that bias actually takes place; Lee et al. found little evidence of routine bias in peer review. Nevertheless, if bias does occur—even on a small scale—it would be preferable to remove the possibility of that bias rather than allowing it to remain. It is perhaps pertinent to ask why triple blind is not more widely used, since the possibility of bias (even subconscious bias) is likely to be an issue for editors as much as for reviewers. The probable explanation is that editors usually like to retain a high level of oversight in the editorial office, whereas triple blind would require them to divest a significant level of oversight to an administrator. Some journals have no administrator other than the editor, so triple-blind review would be impossible to implement.

The major problem identified with double-blind peer review is the practical issue of maintaining anonymity. A survey of 370 chemistry editors and editorial board members found that the most common reason for not adopting a double-blind process was that such protections were perceived to be "pointless" because the identity of the author could be all too easily guessed (Brown 133). Cho et al. found that reviewers were able to identify at least one author for about 40 percent of the papers included in their study. Experience shows that anonymizing papers can be difficult, as it involves not only removing the title page but often removing certain references (if the authors draw attention to their earlier work). Additionally, the name of the research location must be removed, and in some cases, maintaining anonymity requires rewriting certain passages in the third person. Even anonymizing the paper itself might be insufficient, as many submissions begin life as working papers or conference presentations, so that an Internet search on the manuscript title can reveal the author names. Some fields are so specialized that an engaged researcher is likely to know the topics that others in the field are working on and so are likely to make a fair guess about the identity of the author based only on the topic of the paper.

There are other criticisms of double-blind peer review. Various studies have found that using a double-blind process had no effect on the quality of reviews (Ware 17; Goldbeck-Wood; Cho et al.), though Justice et al. did find an improvement in quality. Yet there seems to be no particular reason we should expect double blind to improve the quality of reviews, so this doesn't seem like a pertinent criticism. Another criticism is that hiding the identity of the authors from the reviewers prevents reviewers from raising any conflicts of interest. However, since the reason for raising conflicts of interest is due to potential bias, any such conflicts of interest would be irrelevant if double blind was operating effectively. It is also worth mentioning that under double-blind review, editors and the editorial office can also look for conflicts. Determining conflicts of interest is not solely the responsibility of the reviewer, nor should it be.

Perhaps the only substantial objection to double-blind review, apart from the practical difficulty of operating it, is the assertion that reviewers are limited by not knowing the identities of the authors. Does knowing the identities of the authors prompt the reviewers to ask appropriate questions? For example, it might allow the reviewer to compare the prior work by the authors to determine whether the present submission was new research or derivative (Nature Publishing Group 606). However, one might ask how relevant such questions are for the review process. After all, peer review is not about judging whether the authors have made a substantial advance in their own understanding but whether their submission constitutes a substantial advance for the field.

TRANSFERABLE/PORTABLE PEER REVIEW

One relatively new development in peer review is the idea that authors could, having been rejected from one journal, be allowed to transfer reviews, along with their manuscripts, when they submit to another journal. This does not guarantee that the second journal will not seek further reviews but is intended to speed up the review process and reduce the pressure on reviewers. After all, it is not uncommon for someone to be asked to review the same paper for two different journals.

There are various models for transferable peer review. Some journals, particularly society titles, have one or more "sister" journals that fall within the same broad subject area while having a different focus. An editor might feel that a paper is not suitable for the journal he or she edits but that it would fall within the scope of the sister journal. Another motivation, this time for publishers, is to encourage authors to remain within their "stable" of journals or encourage submissions to their open-access titles. The option to transfer a rejected paper can be attractive to an author if it is perceived as expediting the road to publication elsewhere. Peerage of Science have introduced a new model that operates peer review outside any specific journal. Instead, affiliated journals can look through articles that have already been reviewed and offer to publish them. Another example of "portable" peer review is services offered by organizations such as Rubriq (http://www.rubriq.com/) or Axios (http://www.axiosreview.org). In these instances, papers undergo external peer review and then Rubriq or Axios provide feedback to the authors in an attempt to save time and effort for both authors and journal editorial offices. In some instances, these services might even refer authors to submit their research to a specific journal or set of journals.

One practical problem with transferable peer review is that journals often assess articles by very different criteria, meaning that reviews conducted under the auspices of one journal might not meet the requirements of another. Journals that agree to transfer papers need to have some alignment in their reviewer forms. This variation in standards can also limit the expansion of portable peer-review services if their reviews cannot meet the requirements of potential publications.

Transferable peer review breaks down some of the traditional boundaries in journal publishing, where peer review has often been viewed as something that happens in confidence under the oversight of the journal. Transferability of reviews not only suggests that reviews are a filtering device for that journal but implies a more general statement on the quality of the paper. Transferring reviews also raises some ethical considerations—most pertinently, who owns reviews? There is currently no consensus on this issue. Some authors think journals own the reviews and that reviewers have given their consent to this when agreeing to review; others think that review is a form of privileged communication and therefore still owned by the reviewer (Moylan). Whatever the case, it seems both prudent and honest to be clear with potential reviewers concerning how their reviews will be used. Transferring reviews with papers might break the confidentiality of the review and thus lead potential reviewers to be more reluctant to accept invitations to review.

INDEPENDENCE OF REVIEWERS (COLLABORATIVE REVIEW)

When journals solicit two or more reviews of a paper, they will typically approach the reviewers separately and ask them to produce independent reviews. It is rare for journals to encourage collaboration among reviewers, especially in the context of blind peer review. The rationale for this confidential approach is that two or more reviewers reporting independently can achieve greater objectivity than can the same two or more reviewers coming to a joint conclusion. However, changes in technology have encouraged some journals to try innovative, collaborative approaches to peer review that challenge this status quo.

The European Molecular Biology Organization (EMBO) journals offer reviewers the opportunity to provide feedback on each other's reports. The editorial office then combines these comments into a single report. Another variation is operated by eLife, where there is discussion among reviewers, overseen by an editor, until a consensus emerges and a single report is generated from the discussion. After an initial independent review, Frontiers allows real-time online dialogue among authors and review editors until consensus is reached.

Collaborative review could even be employed as a mechanism to train the authors and reviewers of tomorrow. On the assumption that learning how to deconstruct a paper is a great way to train an author to construct a paper of his or her own, the journal *Headache* runs a monthly virtual meeting whereby the United States–based Fellows in Headache Medicine receive instruction on some aspect of evaluating a paper. Following the signing of a confidentiality agreement, the fellows then review a "live" paper collectively. The review is then written up by the meeting chair, typically a member of the editorial board who possesses both subject expertise and a strong background in methodological design and reporting. The journal reports that the discussion is usually very detailed and results in a very thorough review from multiple perspectives.

Anecdotal evidence is that reviewers enjoy the collaboration these models permit. There is also the perceived advantage that if reviewers collaborate with others, they are more likely to work with care and consideration. Authors also benefit from receiving a single report if it removes the possibility of receiving conflicting recommendations from two different reviewers.

Collaboration can feel more positive and constructive than traditional approaches to peer review. Reviewers and editors might see such collaboration as focusing peer review more on improving the paper rather than seeking reasons to reject it, and while this might seem a worthy aspiration, the reality is that busy reviewers rarely have the time or inclination to be unpaid supervisors for junior researchers. Journals, after all, are not vehicles whereby reviewers educate other reviewers, like heavily supervised student coursework, but vehicles whereby authors are able to disseminate knowledge to readers.

PUBLIC PEER REVIEW

Another new approach to peer review takes advantage of platforms reminiscent of our familiar social media outlets, such as Facebook or comment sections in an online newspaper. Public peer review (sometimes also called "open" peer review) makes the submitted paper available to a large pool of individuals and allows them to add unsolicited comments. This review process has much in common with postpublication peer review (see the following), inasmuch as the paper is made public while the review process is ongoing. The difference between public and postpublication peer review, as we shall see, is that public peer review occurs prior to the publication of a final copyedited and typeset version—the version of record.

Experiments with public peer review have proved less than successful (Björk and Hedlund). In 2006, *Nature* conducted a trial in which authors were asked if they would be willing to have their manuscripts placed on an open server where comments could be placed by any reader. Meanwhile, manuscripts were also reviewed in the normal way. The trial was judged to be a failure. Of 1,369 authors, only 71 (5 percent) agreed to have their papers placed on the open server. Despite healthy traffic on the server, 33 percent of papers received no comments at all. None of the public comments left for the papers were deemed to be particularly significant or to have influenced the decision of the editors. The general reaction to the trial seems to have been indifference: "Anecdotally, potential commenters felt that open peer review is 'nice to do' but did not want to provide any feedback on the papers on the server" (Nature).

Those who run editorial offices will know that editors must typically approach several people before someone assents to review a paper. Reviewers, after all, are trying to fit reviewing into a busy schedule—not least their paid employment—and the more sought-after reviewers are forced to decline invitations quite regularly. Given this response rate for blind reviews solicited by editors, it is unsurprising that the response rate for unsolicited public reviews is so poor. For that matter, editors select reviewers they can trust because of their demonstrated expertise and are not interested in the random comments of those potentially unqualified to review. Here again, it seems unsurprising that the unsolicited comments of public peer review would produce such patchy results.

Björk and Hedlund (2015) raise the additional question of maintaining consistency in the peer review process, suggesting that leaving the review process to the whimsy of unsolicited reviewers does not give equal opportunity for rigorous peer assessment to all submissions (90). Some suggest that public peer review can only work if there is an incentive for reviewers to contribute, such as giving DOIs for published reviews (ScienceOpen) or awarding points for comments (*PeerJ*; Winker 144).

There is an intuitive appeal in the idea of public peer review, making a gesture as it does to the virtues of transparency and a democracy of opportunity for all to be heard, thus exposing manuscripts (in principle) to all peers rather than to a select few. There is, however, a paradox at the heart of public peer review: the point of publication is the dissemination of knowledge and the point of peer review is to determine what is to be disseminated. Public peer review confuses these priorities and potentially leaves neither publication nor reviewing as well off as they found them.

POSTPUBLICATION REVIEW / DYNAMIC ARTICLES

Peer review developed as a prepublication process, essentially as an extension of the editor's decision concerning what should be accepted for publication and what should be rejected (and, more commonly now, what should be revised before acceptance). However, in recent years, there have been calls from some in the research community to change this paradigm in an effort to increase transparency by opening up manuscripts to review *after* publication. Defined broadly, we can say that postpublication review already exists even in traditional journals, through letters to editors, commentaries, and other associated media (Winker 143). However, letters to the editor engage with the published article rather than assessing it or revising it, since traditional journal publishing has sought to maintain the version of record after publication. The status quo does permit some changes to that version of record, such as a retraction if the paper is found to be fraudulent or a correction to be published in a later issue of the journal, but the goal of the publisher is to produce a final and authoritative version of an article.

There have been a number of attempts to encourage postpublication commentary, such as those journals that set up comments pages to accompany articles. Beyond having a comments page, F1000 Prime allows members of the "faculty" to review papers recently published in a variety of journals and provide recommendations to subscribers about what they should read. The F1000 Prime model provides an additional filter for readers, over and above what is selected by editors for publication. A different approach, adopted by PubPeer, allows individuals to post anonymous comments about any published paper. PubPeer boasts some success, having exposed misconduct that has led to the retraction of some papers. On the other hand, PubPeer has also come under criticism for allowing individuals to post anonymously, which might cultivate an environment to "vent spleen at the imperfections of colleagues" (Blatt). Good journals already have policies for dealing with allegations of misconduct in a balanced and confidential manner; it is not clear what advantage there is in posting these allegations to the Internet rather than making them in confidence to the journal.

Postpublication review, more narrowly defined, undertakes peer review after publication either in addition to or instead of prepublication review. An appealing aspect of postpublication review is that it speeds up publication, allowing papers to be placed before the public within days rather than after many months. Another appealing aspect is the transparency of the review process, with readers able to see the manuscript both before and after review. There might also be some appeal in introducing some dynamism into journal publishing, allowing articles to be revised after publication.

But there are also some concerns about postpublication review. What is the status of a published paper that no one has reviewed? Readers have the apparent benefit of immediate access to the paper but no basis on which to determine whether it is worth reading. Researchers already struggle to stay on top of the literature in their fields, so publishing additional papers without any filter would only add to that difficulty. Furthermore, the current model for scientific literature depends on the philosophy that there is a static version of record, an article that can be cited and referred back to. There is a danger that making journal articles dynamic undermines that standard and would require a new understanding of the role of articles in preserving and disseminating scientific knowledge.

One example of this postpublication paradigm is F1000 Research, which brands itself an "Open Science publishing platform." Authors are encouraged to submit their papers, regardless of whether the results are negative or inconclusive. An in-house team checks papers against their basic standards. Assuming everything is satisfactory, the paper is rapidly published online. After publication, invited experts conduct peer review. While the review process is public (or "open"), the reviews are solicited. Articles that pass peer review are indexed in PubMed and elsewhere. The article remains published regardless of the reviewer reports. Authors are encouraged to respond to reviewer comments and publish revisions. F1000 Research is, in some sense, a "halfway house." On the one hand, publication happens before peer review. On the other hand, certain features usually associated with publication (such as indexing) are held back until after review. All versions of the article are citable, including the prereviewed version, but the versions are linked.

Some have argued that allowing articles to be revised postpublication would reduce the flood of scientific papers now being published, since authors would not need to publish new papers that update their findings (Winker 145). However, this misreads the main drivers of publication (i.e., career advancement and research funding) and misrepresents the nature of the scientific literature. Journals are not encyclopedias and articles are not definitive summaries of the state of scientific knowledge. Research articles (as opposed to review articles) report on specific findings and thus are discrete markers along the progress of knowledge. It would be a mistake to confuse the scientific literature for a Wikipedia-style outlet that can be constantly refined and updated.

PEER REVIEW WITHOUT PUBLISHERS

One of the criticisms of peer review, and journal publishing in general, is the role of commercial publishers. Given that peer review differentiates journal content from unfiltered content posted on, say, an Internet blog, undertaking peer review is one way by which publishers add value to submitted content. Obviously publishers themselves do not provide peer review, but they do often provide the infrastructure and underwrite the cost of such review. While publishers usually mandate that editors have editorial autonomy when choosing what to publish, there are still those who are uncomfortable with the role of publishers in peer review. For example, open-access advocate Jan Velterop argued at the Royal Society's Future of Scholarly Scientific Communication Conference in 2015 that the role of publishers should be limited to the technical processes that produce a publishable paper and that peer review should be carried out by the academy (Jump). Ellison (2010) has also speculated that "new institutions may arise and perform many of the same functions as the current peer-review system more efficiently" (657).

There does not currently seem to be much impetus behind such ideas. Academic institutions are not well placed to take on the role of independent peer review. Would they review only the research of their own institutions? In which case, does that constitute independence of review? Or, if some new body is to take on the mantle of peer review, how is it to be funded? Publishers are only able to operate peer review processes because they generate revenue, either through subscriptions or open-access charges. Some other institution would either require public funding or other benefactors who would bring with them their own interests and pressures.

WITHOUT PEER REVIEW

Peer review can slow publication of articles, its operational costs increase the cost of publication, and it is burdensome on reviewers' time. Given criticisms of how effective peer review is, some have argued that science would be better off if peer review was abandoned. Genuine science must be falsifiable, after all, so inevitably what is published will never be unshakable truth. Ultimately it is future observation and experimentation that will demonstrate whether the study was right. Therefore, it might be argued, why try to guarantee the validity of what is published? Just disseminate the paper and let the progress of science determine what stands and falls.

Richard Smith, former editor of the *BMJ*, has argued that it would be left to readers to determine "what matters and what doesn't" (Jump). Some even argue that "peer review has gained its sacred cow status on the basis of little evidence," and there is the further methodological problem at the base of any study on peer review: "How do you assess whether the referee's recommendation is right?" (Smith 10–11).

Another challenge for peer review, which is also a challenge of journals in general, is the ease of dissemination afforded by the Internet. Ellison observes a growing trend in economics for top authors to avoid traditional journals and disseminate by other means. He argues that these authors are able to draw attention to their work, and thus garner citations, by other means. While junior researchers do not have the option to depend on their reputations for readership and citations, there is an increasing use of preprint servers to disseminate articles prior to publication. There is a view that everything should be posted on a preprint server, and then readers would just wait to see what "floats to the top." These preprint outlets allow authors to gain comments and criticism, but their work can also be cited (Curry). These other methods of dissemination challenge the centrality of journals and thus of peer review. Academia is inherently conservative, however, and the current paradigm of academic incentives (career progression, research funding, etc.), either by design or otherwise, helps maintain the centrality of journal publishing.

Despite the criticisms of peer review and the challenges of new models, research suggests that peer review will remain central to journal publishing for many years to come. A recent study of around 3,650 researchers conducted for the Alfred P. Sloan Foundation found that peer review is "increasing its influence" (Nicholas et al. 15). First, peer review is important in determining what should be cited. The study found that researchers are willing to cite conference papers, for example (especially in engineering and computer science), but these conference papers are also not regarded as authoritative (17).

Second, peer review is important for authors in determining where to publish. The study found that peer review was the second-highest criteria, after relevance to the field (Nicholas et al. 17). There is also external pressure to publish in peer-reviewed journals, most obviously to obtain tenure: "The survey revealed that the more prolific the researcher in publication terms, the greater the belief that peer-reviewed journals are the most trustworthy information sources and most prestigious places to publish" (19).

Third, the question as to whether a journal is peer-reviewed is the most important factor for readers in determining what to read, even above personal recommendation or impact factor. Rapid expansion of scientific output has led to researchers gripping more firmly to peer review (Nicholas et al. 21). Researchers will only trust what is disseminated via social media if it is linked to traditional, peer-reviewed sources (19). It is interesting to note that the respondents did recognize the need to assess what they read for themselves—peer review does not confer the status of gospel—but peer review is important for the initial selection of what to read.

The study did find plenty of criticisms of peer review. There were concerns about peer review being slow, about its varying quality, about reviewer bias, and about the lack of transparency, among other things. But there were also concerns about newer models. Some believe that open peer review inhibits reviewers and that postpublication peer review is too easily gamed (Nicholas et al. 16). Repositories, or crowd-sourced peer review (i.e., public peer review), were not mentioned by a single respondent as an option for the future (21). There also seems to be a general uncertainty about the quality of peer review at open-access journals. Yet despite the varied criticisms of peer review, there is still no consensus about how peer review might be improved: "One of the things that struck us was the lack of any plan for a transformed scholarly communication system, even among those who strongly attacked the present one" (21).

Peer review, then, remains engrained in academia, determining where to publish, what to read, and what to cite. Peer review is also central to academic incentives for reputation and progress in one's career; it will not go away until these factors change.

Many of the alternatives to traditional peer review, including scrapping it altogether, are proposed by critics to address specific problems or failings, but it seems that a more basic and fundamental question is often ignored: What is the purpose of journal publishing? Who does it serve? Are journals there to serve the needs and interests of authors, to give them prestige and kudos? Do journals exist to serve publishers or their society owners, to boost subscriptions and/or article processing charges? Do journals exist to serve readers, to provide interesting and informative content? Do journals exist to serve the wider public? Without a clear idea of why we have journals, how can we determine what peer review should do and when it is succeeding?

CHALLENGES FACING
PEER REVIEW

Inevitably, a system that has evolved to serve the world's most inquisitive, informed, and opinionated minds will attract its fair share of scrutiny and criticism. What is so utterly surprising, however, is how little of that comment is actually scientifically validated, based on methodologically rigorous study. Thankfully, research into all aspects of peer review is gradually increasing, though researchers still probably do much of it in their spare time rather than as the primary focus of their careers. There is now a successful quadrennial International Peer Review Congress and a journal (*Research Integrity and Peer Review*) with a specific interest in disseminating research into peer review. The breadth of research output is also broadening from the first works produced, which focused primarily on the mechanism and management of peer review. As Rennie and Flanagin noted, the most compelling issues for study (which also reflect some of the most vocal of ongoing debates surrounding peer review) include the quality of reporting in peer review and publication, transparency and openness, and the need for tools to detect what is real from what is fake (fake research and results, fake peer reviewers, fake journals). To close out this book, it is perhaps worth dwelling on some of the current debates surrounding peer review. Though there is a modernity to the discussion, a result of the disruptive use of technology in peer review, the underlying current to all this chatter remains the same: Should researchers self-regulate, can they do it effectively, and what are the consequences when peer review fails?

MAKING PEER REVIEW MORE SCIENTIFIC

Peer review has been accused of being secretive, open to bias and personal manipulation, and ultimately, an amateurish endeavor (Rennie). The consequences of this are clear (incorrect, invalidated research published; misdirection of future research; potentially negative consequences/harms for patients) and have been discussed elsewhere in this book.

With little evidence to work from, editors—who often ascend to their positions based on their prominence in a given field rather than on the accumulation of years of experience working on journal editorial boards or following specific training—often operate their peer review processes based on anecdote, casual observation, and expediency. As a consequence, what often suffers is the quality of the research published. No wonder John Ioannidis (2005) declared, "Most published research findings are false." This is not to ascribe blame solely to editors. Few are dedicated professionals. Most undertake their work part time. The overwhelming majority operate isolated from outcomes reported in high-level studies into peer review itself and, as a consequence, remain blissfully unaware of data that increasingly show where problems and deficiencies in the peer-review process lie.

In biomedicine at least, perhaps the single most significant debate is now around the issues of poorly reported research, which ultimately frustrates efforts to fully understand whether results presented are real, correct, and free of bias (Moher). Peer review, quite frankly, is failing to detect such problems with consistency (and in the case of a large swathe of titles, failing to undertake any effort to improve reporting standards at all). And here lies possibly one of the biggest failures of peer review: a disappointingly high number of reviewers/journals are not validating results because they simply are not asking authors to better reveal what they did and explain what information/data they included or excluded from the study write-up that constitutes their journal article. In short, if we can't tell exactly what the researchers did, how can we tell if their results are accurate and meaningful?

Ideally, peer review would be better equipped to watch for these issues. That is not to say the tools to better challenge prospective content submitted to journals do not exist. As it approaches 20 years since the publication of the CONSORT Statement (Consolidated Standards of Reporting Trials;

Begg et al.), the first and most important step toward improving the quality of reporting (in this case, for randomized controlled trials), it is still shocking to see that only approximately 600 out of potentially thousands of biomedical journals have bothered to endorse CONSORT, the most well-known reporting guideline produced to date, and execute its requirement that authors better describe their methods. Indeed, not only is there an abject failure on the part of thousands of journals to impose any sort of minimum standards; there seems to be widespread lack of understanding of why journals need to be concerned in the first place.

Journals that do utilize reporting guidelines like CONSORT typically demand that authors improve their reporting either ahead of submission or during the manuscript revision phase. As evidence of the presence of essential reporting elements, many journals ask that authors include a completed reporting guideline checklist with their submissions. CONSORT, for example, uses a 27-point checklist (see http://www.consort-statement.org).

So with a tool such as CONSORT available—which is one of many other reporting guidelines, each designed for different study types and curated by an organization called the Enhancing the Quality and Transparency of Health Research (EQUATOR) Network—and despite repeated examples of poor research slipping past the quality barrier that is supposed to be peer review, why are journals not doing more to preserve the integrity of the published literature and promote better standards?

For a start, editors and editorial boards frequently focus on the perceived *administrative burden* CONSORT and other reporting guidelines place on authors. They perceive that taking the time to go back and include important methodological details and then accounting for them in a summary checklist to aid reviewers is too burdensome; a genuine fear could exist that overworked authors might determine that submitting to journals that impose such standards is simply not worth the effort. In other words, the act of compelling researchers to actually provide the information to facilitate what they should have drilled into them at the start of their careers—that all research is based on validation and replication—is imposing too much on them. Apparently immune to ongoing research into the failures of reporting, let alone the attendant implications, journals maintaining a do-nothing position effectively give tacit approval of an approach to peer review that is little more than a cursory check. Under such circumstances, it seems such journals are content to simply determine that authors are not saying anything too outrageous and ensuring that there are as few as possible impediments to letting authors get published.

At the root of this situation, whereby a sizeable chunk of the published literature cannot be validated or methods cannot be repeated (and is, therefore, arguably useless), is an overwhelming lack of comprehension of the issues of poor reporting and even less of an understanding of why detecting reporting problems is not just a constituent part of peer review but perhaps the single most important part of peer review. Sadly, it seems that journals and reviewers are drawn to the results like moths to a flame while critically overlooking how those results were derived. Yet it is not like these are esoteric or indeed rarefied academic conversational points: most authors would likely attest to frustration after having read a paper from which they could not glean enough information to go back to the lab and repeat. A *Nature* survey even suggested that replication was a major concern for readers (Nature, "Overview"). The situation as it currently stands, and as described previously, represents a collective and overwhelming failure of peer review—doubly so when evidence of the implications of poor reporting and the presence of tools to help correct the problem are well established and readily available.

The failure of peer review to detect reporting problems and in turn spot methodological flaws or the introduction of spin and bias, coupled with a general lack of interest/urgency in addressing the problem, is a very visible failure of peer review. Peer review, it could be contended, is failing to do the job it was set up to accomplish. Some of this failure is built on inertia—a somewhat self-congratulatory belief that despite flaws, peer review works. After all, as a process, it has supported the explosion of research that has ensured there is not a field of academic or scientific study that has not pushed ahead the frontiers of understanding in recent years. Such guilelessness in managing peer review is also derived from a possible collective "arrogance" that buys into and enforces the idea that subject expertise trumps methodological and statistical evidence. Admittedly, that statement immediately falls into the trap we have just condemned—namely, that critiques on peer review are often anecdotal or opinion and not evidence based. However, time and again, political or commercial interests seem to have been prioritized over what surely must have been concerns surrounding the validity of results, especially so at journals where statisticians or experts in study design are retained. This begs the question: In the face of growing evidence that is available and often published in the most prominent journals, such as the *British Medical Journal* (*BMJ*) or the *Journal of the American Medical Association* (*JAMA*), why do editors insist on perpetuating the mistakes of their predecessors by not enacting more rigorous peer review?

So what would a more scientific approach to peer review look like? First, it would use the wealth of evidence and meta-analysis that shows patterns in author behavior and the writing up of research for publication. The most obvious, as discussed, is poor-quality reporting of methods and results. The problem is that most researchers simply are not versed in what constitutes good research practice. This complaint is not new. Doug Altman bluntly summed up the lamentable state of much published research in 1994: "What, then, should we think about researchers who use the wrong techniques (either wilfully or in ignorance), use the right techniques wrongly, misinterpret their results, report their results selectively, cite the literature selectively, and draw unjustified conclusions? We should be appalled."

There are countless examples of what Altman rails against. A classic example is the lack of accounting for post hoc analysis. Researchers all too often do not seem to grasp that it is problematic if you (1) do not publish your originally stated research question, (2) do not describe the outcomes of your investigation of that research question, and (3) decide halfway through your study to answer a new research question that looks more exciting. The flaw with that approach is that the study population was designed to answer the original research question, not the secondary question. Is the population sample now biased? Possibly. What even happened to the original research question? Was there a null or negative result? Why are so few negative or null researched published? Certainly there seems to be an aversion to publishing such material (Franco, Malhotra, and Simonovits). In short, there needs to be a wholesale overhaul in the way research methodology is taught. All too frequently, it is left to (ill-equipped) journals to spot study design flaws. That is already far too late in the process, as the authors simply set off on the wrong path at the start of their study. Somehow peer review is expected to put authors back on the right path. It can be a Herculean task at the best of times and simply impossible on other occasions if the flaw is fatal. Nevertheless, it is remarkable how often such problematic work still eventually surfaces, and not only in obscure titles. In the meantime, and as some sort of palliative, journals can impose policies, protocols, and reporting guidelines and compel their authors to conform. In doing so, problems of bias, spin, unethicalness, and weak study design can be revealed. After that, the journal can take the appropriate action: reject the paper or request changes to remedy the problem.

Another scientific approach to peer review would be through the determination of a set of validated reviewer core competencies, followed by their promotion and accompanied by various training programs. Journals, institutions, or publishers could provide the training. All have a vested interest in training because such efforts should not only elevate the quality of peer review—or at least that is the obvious intention—but also lead those who were trained to better appreciate what is required of them when they in turn become authors. Presently, the Centre for Journalology based in Ottawa, Canada, is among those leading the way to best determine what sort of training reviewers of the future need. Ultimately, the problem will be convincing the very people that need it the most that they should undertake training. There is a concomitant movement to ensure reviewers are better recognized for all their work reviewing a paper, but until the movement succeeds, efforts to provide universal standards in training will be hampered by a lack of motivation for what is a volunteer task that has increasingly been seen to be a burden, as opposed to an honor, in the face of an inundation of research papers. Moher and Altman (2015) propose that we should not stop just at training reviewers. Editors too should be provided with a similar set of core competencies, and potential authors should be trained early on in their careers in the art of writing articles "fit for purpose" (Moher and Altman).

A third, more scientific approach to peer review is the better matching of papers to suitably qualified peer reviewers. Presently, the approach most journals take is that editors simply call on the people they know, have seen speak on a topic, or recall having seen in conjunction with a previously published relevant paper. After that, the online peer review management systems most journals now use might have ways of matching known reviewer areas of expertise with the subject matter for a paper. Such an approach is highly dependent on both the accuracy of the author's description of his or her paper and the accuracy of a potential reviewer's self-awareness of his or her true area of expertise. One such system (ScholarOne) has now started to offer suggested reviewers based on previously published papers, presumably derived from an algorithm that has not yet been subjected to testing or scientific validation. Consequently, it is entirely possible that large pools of potential reviewers, especially in emerging markets, are not being tapped. The smarter selection of potential reviewers is not the only issue surrounding matching of papers to people; evidence in the literature on patterns of acceptance of invitations to review is pretty much nonexistent. At issue is determining whether there is a threshold for reviewer burnout. Most journals are now swamped with submissions, and it is not always the case that their reviewer pools have expanded in a similar fashion. If that is the case, journals are calling on reviewers with greater frequency. Does there come a point when the best-qualified reviewers no longer have the bandwidth to review and thus turn down the invitations with increasing frequency? Then what? Journals start to scramble for less obvious picks and might even resort to calling on people they are unfamiliar with or have not properly vetted, relying on anyone who accepts the invitation to review. Obviously the concern is then that the reviewer is not sufficiently qualified. Another function of burnout is not so much about a growing disinclination to review but the provision of rushed or superficial reviews.

A fourth, more scientific, approach to peer review is through the application of technology. In an ideal world, every journal would be able to call on a cadre of methodological or statistical editors. Realistically, that is unlikely to happen, but in the meantime, solutions are emerging to better detect flaws in methodological reporting, which in turn can be a signpost to bigger issues of poorly conducted studies. One such attempt is through a program called StatReviewer (http://www.statreviewer.com), which at the time of this writing is being piloted on several hundred journals. StatReviewer parses the text of a submission and highlights areas where it feels there are gaps in reporting. Obviously, human intervention is then still required, but the hope is that the software can at least highlight issues both more quickly and with more consistent accuracy than human reviewers, be they trained in methods or simply subject experts. Perhaps we are looking at the early stages of what could be the next great evolution in the assessment of research, particularly with regards to its publication. While there are many inherent weaknesses in humans performing peer review, it seems the addition of training and the development of new machine-based tools might very well raise the bar of peer review.

WHO IS DOING PEER REVIEW?

And so we come to the end of this book by pausing to think about who is doing peer review. As pointed out right from the start, peer review is the manifestation of a community policing itself. But as this book also suggests, the people performing the role are not always qualified, in most cases have never received any training, might not be consistent, might be prone to bias, and are not versed in matters of research methodology, publication ethics, and other issues related to poor author practices. The process of selecting these reviewers is far from transparent and, as journals become increasingly desperate, somewhat scattershot and performed with hope rather than design and intent.

Naturally, in a world where there are more journals (of highly variable quality), more papers, and a lack of a minimum set of standards for peer review, there are many potential gaps that suspect research and dishonest authors can slip through. Consequently, we now live in an age when authors create fake reviewer profiles or spoof actual reviewers to provide fake reviews of their own papers, knowing that many journals are desperate (and careless) enough to simply invite author-suggested reviewers with absolutely no verification procedures. Several large publishers have made more than one purge of papers that were subject to this type of unethical behavior.

In short, it is our opinion that if peer review is to thrive in the face of the rising challenges of a deluge of submissions, potential reviewer fatigue, and the lack of a set of minimum standards, we need to see more of the following:

1. A serious, research community–wide recognition that there are significant gaps not only in the peer review process but also in the training of researchers regarding both study methodology and writing up research for publication. Institutions ultimately have to take responsibility for

this. However, it seems more likely that success will come from elsewhere. Journals, publishers, and scientific and learned societies have a role to play here by holding potential authors to higher standards. Funding agencies also could do more by insisting on standards and withholding future funding if their researchers fail to perform. All these stakeholders can combine forces to help facilitate the development of a universal set of core competencies and a platform from which to teach them. Until there is recognition of a problem and the widespread adoption of a commitment to offer solutions to help all stakeholders raise standards, the same problems will remain. So in discussing who is performing peer review, we could in the future state with authority that it is people who are properly skilled to perform the task.

2. Greater recognition of the invaluable contribution peer reviewers make and the fact that without effort expended, the entire process of scientific and academic publication would either collapse or become a free-for-all with no satisfactory way of validating any research. This does not mean reviewers would receive financial compensation for their time. Despite the vast wealth of many publishers, the economics of journal publishing are such that the overwhelming majority of titles would not be able to fund any peer review. Institutions, however, could shift the paradigm by including peer-review work within any assessments for tenure and promotion. Journals too could do more to recognize the work of their volunteer reviewers. Many do nothing. Some present annual awards to their "top" reviewers and sundry print a list of everyone who performed a review in the previous 12 months. Instead, journals could innovate and invest a little extra effort in order to recognize and reward hardworking reviewers. This could include providing a profile of the reviewer in the journal or maybe a fee waiver for an open-access publication, an expedited publication schedule for any work they submit as an author, or free/discounted publication services. So in discussing who is performing peer review, we could one day reply that it is people motivated by the recognition of those who generously volunteer their time and expertise to assess a paper and further the research in their fields.

3. Be it publishers, societies, or institutions, there needs to be greater deployment of experts with training in methods, statistics, or publication creation. Presently only the most well-resourced journals can offer consistent statistical support. Many authors, unfortunately, are not at institutions that provide their staff with the necessary support, so it might have to fall to others to offer help. The same issue applies to the legion of authors who work in private practice or in nonacademic settings. Conversely, as underresourced as so many institutions are, some are attempting a more enlightened approach (Cobey et al.).

4. Cobey et al. (2016) recently highlighted one effort involving the provision of a publications office role. The concept involves an institution providing a trained individual to all departments to offer guidance on writing up research and navigating the publication and peer-review process. So there needs to be greater recognition of the role of and need for reviewers with specialist knowledge.

5. All stakeholders need to consider the role of technology to either support or replace a human where feasible. Peer review can be cumbersome and lack consistency. A paper might receive a rough review simply because it was assigned to a particular editor who in turn picked tough reviewers. Equally, assigned to a different editor and reviewers, a paper might glide effortlessly through peer review. Peer review should never be, but far too often is, a lottery. Papers must be judged on merit, free from bias and any deficiencies of the reviewers assigned to assess publication worthiness. Perhaps in the future, we can talk about peer reviewers being supported by validating tools that aid their detection of potential flaws.

A FINAL THOUGHT

Nothing within this book will prove revelatory to those who study peer review. Arguably, those engaged in the process for many years either as a prolific author/reviewer or as an editor will equally recognize much of the debate we have recounted. However, such individuals represent the proverbial tip of the iceberg. Overwhelmingly, the players in this game are amateurs, yet the outcomes from their research can represent the highest of stakes—life changing, world changing, history making. Even the myriad small-scale papers that make only the tiniest of incremental change all contribute to the corpus of literature that represents the sum total of understanding of any given field and thus have some value. The reality is that there are thousands of journals, hundreds of thousands of research papers, millions of researchers, and billions of research dollars involved in the process. The smartest individuals on the planet are the stakeholders in peer review and publication. The problems are recognized. The solutions are emerging, if not already available. What is now needed is recognition that the process is flawed but is eminently fixable. There just needs to be the will to do more than passively engage in a process that in its natural resting state might, on a good day, do the job but is otherwise lacking. But the system of peer review is not lacking in potential. The corrective measures are attainable, and when that happens, one can argue that peer review will be more robust than ever. Whether journals will represent the medium for delivering the latest research in the future remains to be seen. Peer review, however, will still be around. Hopefully it will look a little different, and maybe a little healthier, than it does now.

WORKS CITED

Albanese, Mark. "Three Blind Mice—Might Make Good Reviewers." *Medical Education* 40.9 (2006): 828–30. Print.

Altman, D. G. "The Scandal of Poor Medical Research." *BMJ* 308 (1994): 283–84. Print.

"Author Insights 2014." Nature Publishing Group, 2014. Web.

Basken, Paul. "Open-Access Publisher Appears to Have Accepted Fake Paper from Bogus Center." *Chronicle of Higher Education* 10 June 2009. Web.

Begg, C., et al. "Improving the Quality of Reporting of Randomized Controlled Trials: The CONSORT Statement." *JAMA* 276.8 (1996): 637–39. Print.

Biagioli, Mario. "From Book Censorship to Academic Peer Review." *Emergences: Journal for the Study of Media & Composite Cultures* 12.1 (2002): 11–45. Web.

Björk, Bo-Christer. "Have the 'Mega-Journals' Reached the Limits to Growth?" *PeerJ* 3 (2015): n.p. Web.

Björk, Bo-Christer, and Turid Hedlund. "Emerging New Methods of Peer Review in Scholarly Journals." *Learned Publishing* 28.2 (2015): 85–91. Print.

Blatt, Michael R. "Vigilante Science." *Plant Physiology* 169.2 (2015): 907–9. Print.

Bohannon, John. "Who's Afraid of Peer Review?" *Science* 342.6154 (2013): 60–65. Print.

Brown, Richard J. C. "Double Anonymity in Peer Review within the Chemistry Periodicals Community." *Learned Publishing* 20.2 (2007): 131–37. Print.

Burnham, John C. "The Evolution of Editorial Peer Review." *JAMA* 263.10 (1990): 1323. Web.

Butler, Declan. "Investigating Journals: The Dark Side of Publishing." *Nature* 27 Mar. 2013. Web.

Chan, An-Wen, and Douglas G. Altman. "Epidemiology and Reporting of Randomised Trials Published in PubMed Journals." *Lancet* 365.9465 (2005): 1159–62. Web.

Cho, M. K., et al. "Masking Author Identity in Peer Review." *JAMA* 280.3 (1998): 243.

Cobey, K. D., et al. "Report on a Pilot Project to Introduce a Publications Officer." *CMAJ* 188 (2016): E279–E280. Print.

Committee on Publication Ethics. "Code of Conduct and Best Practice Guidelines for Journal Editors." 7 Mar. 2011. Web.

Curry, Stephen. "Peer Review, Preprints and the Speed of Science." *Guardian* 7 Sept. 2015. Web.

Decoursey, Thomas. "The Pros and Cons of Open Peer Review." *Nature* (2006). Web. doi:10.1038/nature04991.

Dougherty, Molly C. "Open Peer Review." *Nursing Research* 53.4 (2004): 213. Print.

Ellison, Glenn. "Is Peer Review in Decline?" *Economic Inquiry* 49.3 (2010): 635–57. Web.

Fitzpatrick, Kathleen. "Planned Obsolescence: Publishing, Technology, and the Future of the Academy." *ADE Bulletin* (2010): 41–54. Web.

Franco, A., N. Malhotra, and G. Simonovits. "Publication Bias in the Social Sciences: Unlocking the File Drawer." *Science* 345.6203 (2014): 1502–5. Print.

Fyfe, Aileen. "Peer Review: Not as Old as You Might Think." *Times Higher Education* 24 June 2015. Web.

García-Berthou, Emili, and Carles Alcaraz. "Incongruence between Test Statistics and P Values in Medical Papers." *BMC Medical Research Methodology* 4.1 (2004): 13. Web.

Godlee, Fiona, Catharine R. Gale, and Christopher N. Martyn. "Effect on the Quality of Peer Review of Blinding Reviewers and Asking Them to Sign Their Reports." *JAMA* 280.3 (1998): 237. Web.

"Go Forth and Replicate!" *Nature* 536.373 (25 Aug. 2016). Web. <http://www.nature.com/news/go-forth-and-replicate-1.20473>.

Goldbeck-Wood, S. "Evidence on Peer Review: Scientific Quality Control or Smokescreen?" *BMJ* 318.7175 (1999): 44–45. Web.

Groves, T. "Is Open Peer Review the Fairest System? Yes." *BMJ* 341.c6424 (2010). Web. <http://www.bmj.com/content/341/bmj.c6424>.

Hames, Irene. *Peer Review and Manuscript Management in Scientific Journals: Guidelines for Good Practice.* Malden, MA: Blackwell, 2007. Print.

Hopewell, S., et al. "Impact of Peer Review on Reports of Randomised Trials Published in Open Peer Review Journals: Retrospective before and after Study." *BMJ* 349 (2014): 4145. Print.

Ioannidis, John. "Why Most Published Research Findings Are False." *PLoS Medicine* 2.8 (2005): n.p. Web.

Jefferson, Tom, et al. "Editorial Peer-Review for Improving the Quality of Reports of Biomedical Studies." *Reviews Cochrane Database of Methodology Reviews* no. 2. (2001): n.p. Web. doi:10.1002/14651858.MR000016.pub3.

———. "Effects of Editorial Peer Review." *JAMA* 287.21 (2002): 2784. Web.

Johnston, Daniel. "Peer Review Incentives: A Simple Idea to Encourage Fast and Effective Peer Review." *European Science Editing* 41.3 (2015): 70–71. Print.

Jump, Paul. "Slay Peer Review 'Sacred Cow,' Says Former BMJ Chief." *Times Higher Education* 21 Apr. 2015. Web.

Justice, A. C., M. K. Cho, M. A. Winker, J. A. Berlin, D. Rennie, and the PEER Investigators. "Does Masking Author Identity Improve Peer Review Quality?" *JAMA* 280.3 (1998): 24. Print.

Kennefick, Daniel. "Einstein versus the Physical Review." *Physics Today* 58.9 (2005): 43–48. Web.

Khan, K. "Is Open Peer Review the Fairest System? No." *BMJ* 341.c6425 (2010). Web. <http://www.bmj.com/content/341/bmj.c6425>.

Kronick, David A. "Peer Review in 18th-Century Scientific Journalism." *JAMA* 263.10 (1990): 1321. Web.

Lee, Carole J., et al. "Bias in Peer Review." *Journal of the American Society for Information Science and Technology* 64.1 (2012): 2–17. Web.

Lu, Yanping. "Peer Review and Its Contribution to Manuscript Quality: An Australian Perspective." *Learned Publishing* 21.4 (2008): 307–18. Web.

Macleod, Malcolm R., et al. "Biomedical Research: Increasing Value, Reducing Waste." *Lancet* 383.9912 (2014): 101–4. Web.

McNutt, R. A. "The Effects of Blinding on the Quality of Peer Review: A Randomized Trial." *JAMA* 263.10 (1990): 1371–76. Print.

Moher, D. "Increasing Value and Reducing Waste in Biomedical Research: Who's Listening?" *Lancet* 387.10027 (2015): 1573–86. Print.

Moher, D., and D. G. Altman. "Four Proposals to Help Improve the Medical Research Literature." *PLoS Med* 12.9 (2015): e1001864. Print.

Moylan, Elizabeth. "Who Owns Peer Review?" BioMed Central (blog) 10 Sept. 2015. Web.

Mulligan A., L. Hall, and E. Raphael. "Peer Review in a Changing World: An International Study Measuring the Attitudes of Researchers." *Journal of the American Society for Information Science and Technology* 64.1 (2012): 132–61. Web.

Nature Publishing Group. "Working Double-Blind: Should There Be Author Anonymity in Peer Review?" Nature.com, 2008. Web.

Nicholas, David, et al. "Peer Review: Still King in the Digital Age." *Learned Publishing* 28.1 (2015): 15–21. Print.

Nielsen, Michael. "Three Myths about Scientific Peer Review." Michael Nielson (blog) 8 Jan. 2009. Web. <http://michaelnielsen.org/blog/three-myths-about-scientific-peer-review/>.

Oransky, Ivan. "17 Retractions from Sage Journals Bring Total Fake Peer Review Count to 250." *Retraction Watch* (blog) 19 Aug. 2015. Web. <http://retractionwatch.com/2015/08/19/17-retractions-from-sage-journals-bring-total-fake-peer-review-count-to-250/>.

"Overview: Nature's Peer Review Trial." *Nature* (Dec. 2006). Web. doi:10.1038/nature05535.

Padula, Danielle. "Possibilities for Peer Reviewer Recognition: ORCID, CASRAI & F1000 Working Group." Scholastica (blog) 25 June 2015. Web.

"Peer Review on Trial." *Nature* 441.7094 (2006): 668. Web.

"Prince of Wales Opens Royal Society's Refurbished Building." Royal Society 7 July 2004. Web.

Rennie, Drummond. "Editorial Peer Review: Its Development and Rationale." *Peer Review in Health Sciences* (1999): 1–13. Web.

———. "Let's Make Peer Review Scientific." *Nature* 535 (2016): 31–33. Print.

Rennie, Drummond, and A. Flanagin. "The Eighth International Congress on Peer Review and Biomedical Publication: A Call for Research." *JAMA* 313.20 (2015): 2031–32. Print.

Rothwell, P. M. "Reproducibility of Peer Review in Clinical Neuroscience: Is Agreement between Reviewers Any Greater than Would Be Expected by Chance Alone?" *Brain* 123.9 (2000): 1964–69. Web.

Shashikiran, N. D. "The Art of Scientific Writing." *Journal of Indian Society of Pedodontics and Preventive Dentistry* 31.4 (2013): 213–14.

Smith, Jan. "Peer Review: A Vital Ingredient." *Serials* 4.2 (1991): 9–12. Print.

Smith, R. "Opening Up BMJ Peer Review." *BMJ* 318.7175 (1999): 4–5. Web.

Spier, Ray. "The History of the Peer-Review Process." *Trends in Biotechnology* 20.8 (2002): 357–58. Web.

Springer. "Retraction of Articles from Springer Journals." Springer Nature 18 Aug. 2015. Web. 11 Jan. 2017. <http://www.springer.com/gb/about-springer/media/statements/retraction-of-articles-from-springer-journals/735218>.

"Striving for Excellence in Peer Review." *Nature Neuroscience* 12.1 (2009): 1. Web.

van Rooyen, S., et al. "Effect of Open Peer Review on Quality of Reviews and on Reviewers' Recommendations: A Randomised Trial." *BMJ* 318.7175 (1999): 23–27. Print.

Walsh, E. "Open Peer Review: A Randomised Controlled Trial." *British Journal of Psychiatry* 176.1 (2000): 47–51. Print.

Ware, Mark. "Peer Review: Benefits, Perceptions and Alternatives." Publishing research consortium summary papers, 2008. Web.

Watkinson, Anthony. "Wiley." Wiley Exchanges 1 July 2005. Web.

Weicher, Maureen. "Peer Review and Secrecy in the 'Information Age.'" *Proceedings of the American Society for Information Science and Technology* 45.1 (2008): 1–12. Print.

Weller, Ann C. "Editorial Peer Review for Electronic Journals: Current Issues and Emerging Models." *Journal of the American Society for Information Science* 51.14 (2000): 1328–33. Print.

Williamson, Alex. "What Will Happen to Peer Review?" *Learned Publishing* 16.1 (2003): 15–20. Web.

Winker, Margaret. "The Promise of Post-publication Peer Review: How Do We Get There from Here?" *Learned Publishing* 28.2 (2015): 143–45. Print.

Xia, Jingfeng. "Who Publishes in 'Predatory' Journals?" *Journal of the Association for Information Science and Technology* 66.7 (2015): 1406–17. Print.

ABOUT THE AUTHORS

Adam Etkin is an established leader in scholarly publishing with more than 20 years of experience and a true passion for the industry. He is highly experienced with all aspects of the STM environment, including submission and peer review, access models, funding mandates, publishing and hosting platforms, ethics, scholarly metrics, and more.

Thomas Gaston is a managing editor in the peer-review management department at Wiley (Oxford), where he supports many journal editorial offices. He has a doctorate from the University of Oxford and has published in books and journals.

Jason Roberts, PhD, is the senior partner at Origin Editorial, a peer-review management company. He is also the former president of the International Society of Managing and Technical Editors. Dr. Roberts has been heavily involved in implementing strategies to improve both the quality of peer review and its effective deployment, with special interest in both biomedical and physics journals. He resides in Ottawa, Canada.

CPSIA information can be obtained
at www.ICGtesting.com
Printed in the USA
BVOW07s1405261217
503650BV00020B/1194/P